CELESTIAL PSYCHOLOGY
An Astrological Guide to Growth and Transformation

DORIS HEBEL

AURORA PRESS

205 Third Ave.   2A   New York, N.Y. 10003

Also by Doris Hebel

CONTEMPORARY LECTURES:
Chart Interpretation, Astrology and Psychology, Relationships

First published in 1985 by
Aurora Press
P.O. Box 573
Santa Fe, N.M. 87504

ISBN: 0-943358-18-3
Library of Congress Catalogue Card No:
84-072405

Dedication

*To Barbara, my
friend and
publisher without
whom this book
would not be.*

ACKNOWLEDGEMENTS

It's really impossible to salute everyone who has had an important influence in one's professional development, so forgive me if I don't mention you by name.

Earliest in my career, even before it was a career, Julie Baum encouraged me. Indeed, since her Sun conjuncts my Aries Uranus she insisted that I go public with lectures and consultations.

Countless books and lectures made their impact and the most significant books were those of Europeans. The work of Reinhold Ebertin opened new possibilities since I'd been struggling against accepting my feeling that the nature of the aspect was not what defined positive or negative. Alfred Witte's work, called Uranian Astrology in the United States, for its preciseness and added perspective about the planets.

To my editors Brian Emo and Ann Parker. Without their work of pulling together various pieces of my information I couldn't have handled the job of getting this book done.

And most importantly my thanks to all those students of life, my clients, students and colleagues whose willingness to share their observations and experience have indescribably enriched me.

TABLE OF CONTENTS

INTRODUCTION

Why did I write this book? The purpose of an introduction is really to answer that question. My answer is: to provide some alternative perspectives on how to handle the planetary energies.

When I began studying astrology in the late 1950's I could not find information on how to manage various aspects. The hidden message in the books I read was one that perpetuated the idea of "fate," that there wasn't anything you could do about it.

I've always believed that there are bound to be some solutions to problems and I looked on difficult planetary connections as problems to be solved rather than curses! My perspective has been that we are responsible for ourselves and our lives whether we like it or not, and although I believe in karma and reincarnation, I consider the life circumstances we bring on ourselves as opportunities to grow rather than punishment for mistakes or "crimes." Most Westerners raised in the Judeo-Christian ethic who later accept the ideas of reincarnation usually unconsciously transfer their guilt or punishment indoctrination to the new belief system.

At any rate, thus began my search for ways to assist change and growth in people's lives through their tough aspects rather than in spite of them.

When I began studying astrology there was only one teacher in my city and she actively preferred that Capricorns (I am one) not take her classes. At the time my burning need to know was outraged, but it did turn out to be the best thing that could have happened for I was forced to learn on my own. My mother had studied Astrology. She suggested readings and taught me how to calculate. I read lots of the books available (by no means all, and I didn't discover Rudyhar until the 1970's) and then my friends insisted I do their charts. In doing so, I quickly discovered that much of the material on planetary aspects didn't fit the experience of my friends or my knowledge of them. I was still working as a professional librarian at the time and had a long-term love affair with books. It was hard for me to accept that most of the information in these books wasn't pertinent to the lives of those I knew, but it was true.

i

Since then I've developed some theories about this. First, the consciousness of an individual, group, nation or time period conditions how the planetary energy is felt and expressed. What may be true for a certain person or group of people during a specific time in history is not true for others. Second, authors and lecturers are human and do not always include their own original research or observations. Therefore old perspectives become perpetuated. Third, the examples, used by many astrologers in their books and lectures, are the most dramatic, not necessarily reflecting the way most people will experience the planetary energy.

My friends continued to contribute to my learning astrology from the ground up since I asked them to keep diaries of events, attitudes, etc., which I matched with the natal, progressed and transiting planets. Then my friends began insisting that I read charts for others and after several years' resistance, I gave in. That was in 1967. Since 1968 I've been making my living as a full-time counseling astrologer, teacher and lecturer.

How come it took so long for this first book to come out? Well, lazy and scared cover it—and one of the more compelling reasons was that I couldn't possibly include everything. My Sun-Mercury-Mars-Saturn had a really hard time with that! When my publisher got through to me that I didn't have to include everything, the project really took off.

This book is not comprehensive! This is a warning to you, the reader—don't expect to find every iota of information on a particular planetary contact or, indeed, everything that fits your own personal experience. Astrologers are not ordinary people—mostly we're mavericks—so we may react differently to many run-of-the-mill circumstances in life.

The information in this book comes from listening to my clients, most of whom are urban middle-class professionals; and, from my counseling experience. The information reflects their concerns and often their solutions. When I've suggested ways to handle energies based on my perceptions of how the planets work, and when my clients have found these solutions worked, I've included them.

Modern daily issues of life need to be addressed by the astrologer in order to counsel adequately. Value judgments should be rooted out ruthlessly. Getting entrenched in old perspectives limits sensitivity to issues and situations. To expect, for instance, that a certain planetary contact always produces a particular result is to deny the validity and variety of human experience and to ignore one's ability to alter the impact of the planets by one's own consciousness. Most astrologers seem to be convinced of the inevitability of the particular effect of the planets. What I've found is that people are truly remarkable in their abiliity to manifest the nature of the planets and signs in keeping with their basic meanings and to add richness and nuance beyond what anything most astrology books hint.

Astrologers should struggle against the natural tendency of "the expert" to become intellectually arrogant. Always consider that you may be wrong and give the clients a chance to express themselves— you'll only be richer for it and will become better equipped to counsel others.

Doris A. Hebel
Chicago, Ill.
December, 1984

CHAPTER 1

A PERSPECTIVE ON ASPECTS

There is currently much confusion among both students and professional astrologers regarding the quality and power of astrological aspects. It is not the 'aspect,' I believe, that defines positive and negative influences in the birthchart; rather it is the 'nature' of the planets forming the aspect. The energy of a particular planet will combine harmoniously with some planets, less comfortably with others. This point of view is one of the basic principles underlying both the Uranian and Cosmobiology systems of astrology, and it is an idea that I have found applies to any system of astrology. For instance, with a Venus/Saturn aspect, Venus is helpful to Saturn but Saturn has a repressive influence on Venus. A trine between these planets represents the same fundamental energy as a square, although the level of intensity is significantly different. Hard aspects between antithetical planets in air/fire charts seem to produce about the same level of intensity as soft aspects between the same planets in earth/ water charts. A person's background, conditioning and location also play a part in how intensely a contact is felt. For instance, two people with identical charts—one living in New York City, known for its hustle and bustle, and the other living in Santa Fe, New Mexico will naturally be "tuned" and react differently from each other.

We are accustomed to thinking of trines and sextiles as good, squares and oppositions as unconditionally bad. That is simply not true. The 45-degree aspect series (conjunction, semi-square, square, sesquiquadrate, and opposition) are considered "hard" aspects. Hard, in this case, doesn't mean difficult; it means 'hard' angle, which comes from the idea of a square or right angle. (The quincunx, even though it is not a member of the 45-degree aspect series, can be considered a difficult aspect, one needing adjustment between two planetary energies.) What these aspects are then is 'intense,' not necessarily hard. They indicate that something is going on inside which is so intense that it manifests externally in a person's life.

The 'soft' sextiles and trines, which tend to be less intense, pose their own special kind of problem—they manifest energy primarily on the internal level. I call them the "If only . . ." aspects. "Wouldn't it be nice if only . . ." or "I know I could do this if only . . . "For instance, a Mercury/Neptune soft aspect says, "I would really like to travel sometime, wouldn't it be nice if only . . ." Soft aspects can be difficult simply because the energy exchange is not intense enough to manifest on the physical plane. We can't seem to produce tangible results.

In this book, interpretations can also apply to midpoints and parallels which are also considered contacts between planets or groups of planets.

An excellent way to test the 'nature' vs. 'aspect' emphasis is to start with your own chart. Select any soft or hard aspect, then refer to any astrological text and read all the different aspect delineations involving the two planets. If you have a Mercury/Saturn aspect, read everything written on the conjunction, sextile, square, trine and opposition. You will notice that all the interpretations, hard and soft, seem to describe your own experience of the two planets. This should ease your mind about all the so-called death, doom and damnation aspects in your own or someone else's chart. When I started studying astrology many years ago, I read all the available books on the subject. Unfortunately, most of these older texts are filled with what I call 'wrist slitters' statements. Based on these interpretations alone, if you have mostly "hard" aspects, you are worthless and nothing good will ever happen to you. For instance, Sun square Mars denotes a person with a violent temper who is capable of murder or who will be murdered; physical violence is endemic to the aspect. I have Sun squaring Mars in my own chart, and, although I have been angry at times, I have not seriously entertained the thought of killing someone. Obviously, no one has yet killed me. Nor do I continually encounter violence.

This sinister interpretation has its roots in the historical perspective of people who lived centuries ago. In simple terms, Sun/Mars aspects mean self-motivation. But in the dark ages, when a majority of people were literally serfs or slaves with little power to direct their own lives, a serf with a self-assertiveness of Sun square Mars would probably have been beaten or killed. In that society, a Sun/Mars square wasn't very auspicious. Today, the self-motivation of this aspect is considered to be very useful in directing your life.

We are attuned by our planetary contacts to select, without the conscious application of will, only those experiences or mental assumptions that "fit" the raw meaning of our planets. Youngsters absorb and collate. Only later, as teens or adults, when we start directing ourselves, do our planetary contacts show their potential.

Initially, we concentrate on playing out mostly the difficult side of our planetary contacts, either because we aren't encouraged to do otherwise or because we stubbornly choose to ignore or discount the positive side. An example is a third house Saturn person. This individual retains the conditioning from childhood that warns "be careful," "don't trust," "don't believe everything you read or hear," etc. This person probably also had people around who said "look on the bright side," "nothing ventured, nothing gained," and generally promoted being upbeat. But, those are not the attitudes that "stick" to a third house Saturn person without conscious effort.

If we are on the path of growth, we begin to select, with the conscious application of will, the fuller expression of our planetary contacts and we can then include more of the positive meaning. This world is the plane of Saturn, and we need to learn before we can truly benefit. This is most likely why that ancient Saturn truism still holds that things get better as we get older.

Modern astrologers are in a constant process of recodifying astrological information to make it more pertinent in today's world. Aspects must be studied on an empirical basis by examining their characteristic expression in both the internal and external areas of life. Only then, is it possible to deduce their attributes.

Throughout this book, the words "aspect" or "contact" will indicate any and all possible connections between two planets, unless a specific type of aspect is mentioned. Even the supposedly minor aspects such as the semi-square, sesquiquadrate, inconjunct, quintile, biquintile and septile should be considered as important aspects. Midpoints, parallels and contraparallels (aspects in declination) are also quite powerful. Remember, it is the level of intensity or challenge to action that is amplified or mitigated by the angle of the aspect, not the intrinsic energies of the planets. These remain the same.

The time periods in life ruled by the planets can also give us a clue as to when the influence of the planet is most strongly felt, or when we can make efforts to alter our programming (other than those times shown by transits and progressions).

PLANETARY TIME PERIODS

Moon	Birth through age 6
Mercury	7 through 13
Venus	14 through 20
Sun	21 through 27
Mars	28 through 34
Jupiter	35 through 41
Saturn	42 through 48
Uranus	49 through 55
Neptune	56 through 62
Pluto	63 through 70

A quick look at this listing reveals some interesting points. The Venus period is when the body matures, hormones flow, we start to date and to experience stronger sexual urges. The Mars period is when one "stakes a claim" in the world and begins working toward it more consciously. The Neptune period often heralds a dissolution of health and/or a return to religious or spiritual values. The end of the Pluto period corresponds with the average life span. Before the discovery of Pluto the average life span was about 62 years in the United States.

When a person reaches age 71 we can start over again at the top of the list. This need not be the negative "second childhood" but rather a renewed blossoming of the personality and an increasing growth. It is up to each person to live life fully and to alter the inhibiting attitudes and structures of society for the common good.

CHAPTER 2

SATURN

Saturn is the planet of time, structure, reality, commitment, mastery, restraint, withholding, guilt, repression, discipline, rigidity, limitation, denial, fear, sadness, withdrawal, separation, and, finally, wisdom. Note that 'wisdom' comes at the end of this list; it is earned only after we have mastered fully the lessons Saturn intends to teach us. Saturn, the cosmic lawgiver, the cosmic law itself, embodies personal duty and responsibility. If we creatively use Saturn to learn these lessons in our lives, we can reach the highest level of conscious awareness—wisdom. When the ancient philosophers referred to our 'wisdom' teeth (those received later in life),the implication was that we didn't learn anything valuable without some degree of pain. And Saturn does extract its quota of pain. It is often only in sorrow and anguish that we are challenged to transcend our present limitations, life circumstances, and boundaries to advance beyond inertia. Only in attempting to navigate life's more difficult crises points are we compelled to learn about our true selves.

Our concept of reality, our experiences, our ego-centered consciousness—all are shocked and shaped from birth as Saturn seeks to establish our unique and authentic identity. All the negative aspects of Saturn within the personality seem to stem from one major premise — separation. Separation is basically what Saturn signifies. Apparently, it is the jarring separation from the mother at birth that unconsciously motivates us to overdramatize and overplay our separateness, to feel that life must be a continual process of abandonment and loneliness. In modern times, the birth separation has been made even more traumatic with harsh lights, drugs and placement in a nursery to cry alone. Children, lovable though they may be, are egocentric little savages (remember how you were?). They feel they are the centers of their universe, that everything revolves around them, so if something bad is going on, it must be their fault. Thinking you aren't "good enough" is typical of Saturn. But as adults, we can learn from Saturn. Having a philosophical framework that includes reincarnation and karma, I believe that Saturn shows us the direction of our karmic duty and responsibility. The Signs and Houses occupied or ruled by Saturn, as well as its aspects, disclose the areas of experience and the types of people with whom we feel most vulnerable; where needs must be filled and special attention given; where Saturn threatens our concept of self-importance and value. An angular position of Saturn works in an even more intense and demanding fashion, insisting constantly that one must learn and grow.

As "lord of karma," Saturn points to our capacity for free will in determining the course of our lives. It is by paying our dues, consciously working through our karmic lessons, that we can attain true freedom and power of choice. Feeling blocked or frustrated in any situation results from rigidly and stubbornly trying to maintain control against all odds, and refusing to deal flexibly with a problem. Reality, in terms of this material plane, is telling us to learn a new way, often hard won, to deal successfully with our lives. This is the higher form of Saturn.

Retrograde and intercepted Saturn placements are similar in their effects — holding back, creating self-conscious subjectivity, sensitivity, the feeling of incompleteness. It is difficult to get a positive perspective on this type of Saturn. It makes us feel that no matter how hard we try or what action we take, it will turn out rotten. The retrograde motion indicates a situation is being repeated as part of a karmic pattern. The sense of fatalism grows out of the feeling that the situation is beyond our control. In actuality, it isn't. We simply passed over a previous opportunity to live constructively, so now we must become more aware of necessary lessons to be learned in this lifetime.

An intercepted Saturn increases our emotional sensitivity, contributing to withdrawal from life. Though acutely aware of the energy present, it is as if a person feels he must 'break down walls' in order to use it. These feelings of entrapment can sometimes be alleviated by relocating physically. Although the natal chart continues its influence, the relocation can give a new emphasis for planetary energy. To achieve this new and broader perspective provided by the rearrangement of Saturn energies, a person must incorporate both the natal and relocated Saturn functions, which means combining the activities of the two houses involved, as well as the two houses ruled by Saturn.

Saturn is the Great Teacher. Saturn people can change in spite of their initial belief that they can't, that it's not worthwhile or that it won't work anyhow. Accompanying the internal scare that change is likely to be bad, is the quieter, stronger hope that this isn't so. Whether Saturn people change because they're tired of the way things are or because those who love them keep requiring them to change, they usually begin to lighten up after age 30. This process, however, must begin before age 45; it is increasingly difficult to change later. Those who successfully change after 45 are usually strongly Plutonian.

SATURN CYCLES

Saturn, in the role of timekeeper, makes us feel limited, denied. It's not that Saturn really denies, it's just that it takes so long for something to happen that it feels like denial. Saturn will not reward or grant us something simply because we think it's time to receive it. Saturn makes us work for it. Though most of us are aware of the issues needing to be addressed, we often seduce ourselves into thinking these can be evaded or sidestepped. They can't. Saturn reminds us of our responsibility to deal with unfinished business before we can hope to reap any benefits. Ultimately, we are rewarded, but only when Saturn dictates the time is right. We haven't been denied anything. But we may have delayed our own prosperity, happiness, or growth by refusing to confront the unresolved problems which are blocking our fulfillment.

Saturn, in the natural zodiac, is related to the meridian axis. If we assign Aries to the 1st house, Capricorn (the sign ruled by Saturn) will appear on the 10th house cusp. Uranian astrologers place Libra on the Ascendant, which puts Capricorn on the 4th house cusp. Using either system will result in Saturn's affiliation with parents. Reality dictates that even if highly sensitive people regard a "key" parent as 'bad' or 'difficult' there is still something positive and useful to be learned through the relationship.

The First Saturn Return
The first return of transiting Saturn to its birth position, between the ages of 28 and 30, is a time of maturation. Life prior to the return has a quality of eagerness and lightness. We express our energies in a myriad of ways, exploring choices and pathways in a continual process of trial and rejection. Then, during the return, we begin to feel pressured to grow up; life seems less free. We are being required to toe the line, clean up the messes of our previous behavior, commit ourselves to something (whether it concerns home life, job, or health), and then single-mindedly pursue it in spite of the fear of failure. At this time, people often find that certain circumstances in their lives seem to block the growth required. Some may leave limiting jobs for new ones. Marital relationships, based on unrealistic expectations, frequently break up. Others marry or have children at the return as an expression of their willingness to accept commitment.

An angular birth placement of Saturn, triggered by the return, will force people to deal with numerous unresolved issues in their lives. The succedent and cadent placements may foster ambivalence about confronting issues. But, wherever Saturn is placed, if correct action is not taken during the return, Saturn may provide a rude awakening at the next opposition or even the first square.

After the first Saturn return, we can exchange a multiplicity of options for a well-defined field of action. Life begins to have greater meaning; the existential pieces of the puzzle start falling into place. People often feel more 'connected' to life and more committed to being on the planet.

The Second Saturn Return

At the second return, occurring in a person's late 50's, we survey the results of our action or inaction, our adult behavior or lack of it. The possible tragedy of this period may be the recognition of failure, of not doing the "job" the way we intended, of having lost this time and its possibilities forever. If you read the obituaries, you will note how many people die in their late 20's and 50's. It is as if, in the late 20's, the soul knows that the present personality cannot fulfill the growth required, and in the late 50's, death is the expression of the greatest form of self punishment for not having lived up to one's true potential.

The First Saturn Opposition

The first Saturn opposition to natal Saturn occurs at approximately age 14. We can all recall how perfectly miserable we were in our early teens, struggling to take charge of our lives in a society that still labeled us children. There would be less trauma at the first Saturn, if youngsters, going through the first Saturn opposition, were allowed to make some of their own decisions about their lives and to deal with the consequences of these decisions. A teenager who chooses to be late to school every day (having been given the freedom to determine his own schedule) should have to answer to the school authorities directly; parents shouldn't be responsible for the teenager's behavior. In this way, the teenager learns directly what his choices ultimately cost and is better prepared to function in the world.

The Second Saturn Opposition

The second opposition of transiting Saturn to the natal Saturn occurs at about age 44. At this stage in life, with many domestic responsibilities largely over, people are freer to pursue personal goals. Saturn begins to grant some of the 'goodies' that were formerly withheld because of other responsibilities. This can be a time of increased enjoyment and satisfaction. Conversely, in a negative manifestation of Saturn, some people voluntarily trap themselves in what they continue to see as their "responsibilities." Women with older children may limit themselves by trying to cling to the mother role. (Saturn is symbolically involved with the Moon, the angles, the 4th house ruler or planets in the 4th house).

At the second Saturn opposition we decide, literally, whether we should live or just exist. It doesn't matter how many years it takes for the physical body to die, a person symbolically dies if he hasn't freed himself of outlived structures, and been true to his essence. Those who decide to "live" fully in the future continue to confront themselves, while those who decide otherwise quickly settle into a life script of increasing dullness, however cushioned it may be with material safety and security. Saturn crystallization gets out of hand and, for there to be any growth, the outer planets may then manifest in very difficult or unpleasant ways to wake us up.

Sometimes a person will have to wait 14 or 15 years to see the benefits of a particular endeavor. Then it comes suddenly at the culmination phase of the cycle when Saturn opposes its original position. Though it is hard to see, this time has allowed for the proper stages of development to unfold so goals can be realized.

Many people today feel an increased sense of burden at the second opposition, even though children no longer need as much supervision, and careers seem to run themselves. Some strike out at those who expect them to behave responsibly. Marriages may end, people may quit jobs—all in a search for freedom while there's still time to enjoy it. Obviously, this won't work. True enjoyment of freedom can only be purchased with the hard work of living one's life responsibly. If people don't add new energy to their life streams at this time through new forms of self-expression, new mental horizons to be conquered, then retirement may bring immediate illness or even death. We must always be open to new opportunities to fulfill the greatest potential of Saturn—mastery, commitment and wisdom. The happiest and healthiest older people are those who are active mentally and physically. And, this is something which must be cultivated throughout life, not at the last possible moment.

The Opening Saturn Square

The opening squares of Saturn to birth Saturn occur at the approximate ages of 7, 35, and 64. Age seven marks a times of separation from home in the form of going to school. Many children go to preschool at the semi-square for socialization, rather than academic purposes, but either of these can represent the first separation from family or familiar environment. This is the first step in maturation, in being out in the world. At about age 35, one is challenged to see if the choices made and action taken at the return are working effectively. Many people feel that if they work hard enough now, they can accomplish what they didn't attempt during the Saturn return and this often is possible. At age 64 many are facing retirement from jobs. Those, whose identity has been defined only by their work, may either die literally or symbolically by dwindling into inertia. At the time of the Saturn opposition, when they are in their mid-40's, people should be encouraged, sometimes pressed, to find additional areas of self-expression so that when they face retirement, they don't need to be added to the still-living but non-functional population. It is unfortunate that, collectively, most of us reject the elderly, when, in fact, the wisdom and knowledge gained by people during their lives can be of benefit to all of us at this cycle.

The Closing Saturn Square

The closing Saturn square occurs at ages 21 and 50. Age 21, recognized as the time of adulthood in western society, marks another separation. Many finish college or live on their own for the first time, experiencing the intense fear of not making the right choices. As with all Saturn transits, the most efficient way of dealing with life at this time is to handle what is immediately in front of you—your job, paying bills, managing your time.

At age 50, one reaches the point in life where western culture bestows the honored position of mentor. There is a great deal of satisfaction in being recognized for having done something well enough to be looked to for advice and guidance. Yet, there's also the bittersweet awareness that there are fewer years ahead than behind. Time and energy now seem too valuable to be squandered on activities or people who don't contribute to one's essence. Although people may have felt guilty about this earlier in life, at this stage they can claim the right to define the use of their own time and energy without excuses to the world.

SUN/SATURN

The Sun and Moon As Parental Indicators

The Sun represents primary masculine energy; the Moon, primary feminine energy. Therefore, I use these as the biological indicators for the parents in the birth chart. (Saturn is, in some charts, very much the father—usually when it is in strong aspect to the Sun or in the 10th house. I use the 4th house for Mom and the 10th for Dad, unless the client says otherwise.) Sun and Moon are of primary importance from birth until the first Saturn square to natal Saturn at age seven. During this seven-year period, Sun and Moon come to represent the child's evolving attitudes, behavior and belief systems concerning men and women. The primary male is usually Dad; the primary female, Mom. The unconscious mind apparently does not distinguish minutely between people. It views all males as Dad and all females as Mom, never mind what the conscious mind is saying. So important is this seven-year period that many adults spend years clearing up and redefining these early perspectives, especially after one or two unsuccessful love relationships. The astrology chart is a reflection of the *self* in all areas of experience, including relationships. Most of us insist on seeing the *other* person as separate from *self*, when in reality we attract only those who mirror dynamically that which we persistently evade or cannot deal with in ourselves. Once we acknowledge and accept these uncomfortable facts, our interactions with others often alter dramatically.

In a birth chart with Sun/Saturn contacts, the resonant glory of the Sun is denied full expression. The person either is denied enough time (Saturn) to bask in the glory of the Sun, represented by the father, or experiences only the negative aspects of the masculine personality. *Lack* is the major awareness—lack of attention, acceptance, approval, and acknowledgement. It may be that the father's business or professional activities prevent his spending more time with the child, or the separation may be caused by outside factors. Unfortunately, children do not recognize these outside pressures as real. They interpret them, rather, as lack of interest or love, for which they often blame themselves. This is the root of the *ambition* of the Sun/Saturn personality. Achieving an ambition is actually the person's way of wrenching from the world the approval withheld, denied or doled out by the father. Sun/Saturn persons believe that no matter how hard they try, their effort will never be enough to gain Dad's approval. The fathers are usually very reserved and any praise is only "heard through the grapevine." Dad tells Mom, or someone else, who tells the Sun/Saturn person. Dad may only be able to express praise directly by bluff joking. As an adult, the Sun/Saturn person can often achieve approval from Dad by unbending enough to confess feeling unloved, unwanted or abandoned. If this is done without whining, the father may relate his pleasure and approval of the Sun/Saturn person's behavior over the years. The hitch in the whole thing is that Sun/Saturn persons are so convinced they will meet further criticism and rejection that they will rarely allow themselves to be vulnerable. It is, however, the task of the Sun/Saturn person to take the first steps to heal the breach. Until this breach begins to heal, most important interactions with other men will continue to reflect the initial experiences of separation and denial. Sun/Saturn persons will continue to believe they don't deserve to be loved. If they are connected with a warm, outgoing man, they will often discount the validity of the relationship, suspect the other's intentions, or behave in a cold, distant way themselves, thus eliciting the very reaction they have convinced themselves is the only thing they deserve.

The father, in reality, may not have been prepared physically, mentally, emotionally or even economically to support a child. He may not have been mature enough to contribute directly and fully to this soul's growth. The sense of isolation engendered by this early life experience stays with Sun/Saturn people throughout their life; and, is something that can be burdensome as they gain authority in the world, which, typical of Saturn, often occurs later in life.

Karmic Implications in Childhood Development
Through hypnotic regression in psychotherapeutic work, some Moon/Saturn people while still in the mother's womb, have reported feeling the mother's apprehension about having a child. Although the actual causes of the apprehension may have nothing to do with the child, having been determined generally by the mother's life circumstances, Saturn contacts with the Sun or Moon (or in angular houses) do seem to imply that birth occurred at a difficult time—whatever the reasons. This does not mean the parents didn't want, love and cherish their child. One of the enormous break-

throughs in a person's counseling occurs with the realization that the circumstances surrounding birth were beyond the control of both child and parents.

On a karmic level, Sun/Saturn or Moon/Saturn contacts in the birth chart can indicate that these people have been, in a previous lifetime, biological or symbolic parents to one of their present parents. As children, they may sense that their parents, in this lifetime have again placed them in a parental role (the relationship as it was structured in a former lifetime). Feeling they are expected to be "grown-up" they rise to the responsibility to obtain approval and love. They comply with parents' demands and behave like good little girls or boys. As adults, they may feel bound to take care of their parents even to the event of living with them and postponing their own lives. The parents in this case have not been able to relinquish control and may even use guilt-inducing means to hang onto the adult/child.

The parents of Sun/Saturn or Moon/Saturn children may place too heavy a burden of responsibility on them, denying them many opportunities to experience the kind of childhood that literature, cinema and television have seduced them into believing they should have. But when these children exercise the freedom they feel should accompany their responsibility, the parents may suddenly become aware of the children's actual age and often restrict their activity. A struggle for control results, one that is most noticeable when children reach age seven — at the first Saturn square to Saturn — even earlier if these planets are angular or rule angular houses. This problem would not occur if children were not encouraged to accept responsibility beyond their years, or if freedoms and rewards were also granted.

The parents of Saturn children may answer efforts for approval with harsh or unfair criticism. Depending on their sensitivity, the children may become depressed by the condemnation, retreat within themselves, or even lose hope of ever doing enough to please the parent. A preponderance of Air/Fire in the birth chart is not as intensely sensitive as a heavy concentration in Water/Earth. However, if Sun/Saturn or Moon/Saturn falls in Air/Fire along with a concentration of personal planets or points in Water/Earth, the person will continue to respond with greater sensitivity to the parent.

One of the negative qualities of Saturn is its tendency to fix blame. Sun/Saturn or Moon/Saturn people often spend years blaming their own shortcomings on their parents' lacks and insensitivity. Until these individuals stop blaming others, they can't begin their own personal growth. The karmic implication is that the soul has correctly chosen the parents and that the individual needs to meet his/her destiny. Esoteric astrologers often speak of Saturn individuals as "old souls." This may be true, but they are old souls who have yet to grow into full mastery. The anguish of the current life can precipitate the next needed step in growth.

The parent-child reversal syndrome can be alleviated if the parent rewards the child with affection for assuming responsibility and making decisions. Children with Saturn contacting their Sun or Moon need positive support from the parent indicated, and this should be given without the child having to "achieve" something to earn it. If Saturn is retrograde in the natal chart, the current roles of child/parent may be a continuation from the previous incarnation. These individuals may be acting out the same script to resolve any residual karma with which they have not dealt adequately in the past.

If we consider Saturn in the spiritual-philosophical sense of karma, it is ultimately the responsibility of the Sun/Saturn or Moon/Saturn individual to rectify the problem with the parent. Especially advantageous times for doing this are either during the progressed Lunar or Saturn return or when Saturn is transiting the Sun or Moon. The individual should then review the past relationship with the parent and determine whether past assumptions and behavior are appropriate to the present situation. It is the time to release negative feelings about the early home life and to begin to relate with the parents as an adult. Some people may experience resistance to this because of their belief that they will never receive the acceptance and approval they need from the parent. However, when the person does begin to relate with the parent on an adult basis, the father and mother are usually delighted and begin to release their own feelings of being rejected by the child. As the destructive bonds are broken, the negative karmic energies are dispersed and new space is created for a more productive relationship.

This new parental acceptance and understanding will enable a person to make dramatic changes in relationships with other men and women. On an unconscious level, all men refer to the father image, all women to the mother image. Once false assumptions about parental relationships have been acknowledged and changed, these people free themselves to rise up in an ever-growing spiral of relationships. Old problems are inevitably faced again in new relationships, but they can be handled more easily because the root problem with the parents has been resolved.

Therapeutic Techniques

The Sun represents the physical vehicle (body). In the charts of both men and women, it is pure vitality and life force. Through its rulership of Leo, the Sun refers to the heart and spine. Aspects from Saturn to the Sun inevitably produce some rigidity in the spine or bony structures, disturbing the balance of other bodily organs. It is important to release this tightness and keep the spine as supple as possible. There are many ways to accomplish this, and Saturn people feel most comfortable with activities they can perform on their own. Since they have difficulty trusting others, they feel they should not allow themselves to be vulnerable, even though they may receive needed benefit from others. Possible exceptions are consulting doctors, dentists or others who can prove their expertise or who have been practicing long enough to mitigate to some degree the lack of trust found with Saturn. It is preferable, initially, for Saturnine people to help themselves as much as possible. To release tightness (not letting go) in the body, try yoga, swimming or dancing, concentrating especially on slow, sinuous, disciplined movements. Rigorous exercise is not effective because its *contract-release* movement promotes even more tension. Saturn makes the body feel too tight; that is what needs to be eliminated. Yoga is one of the most useful disciplines, promoting suppleness in the spine by assuming specific positions designed to realign the body's physical energy.

After completing as much work as possible by oneself, allow another person to work on the body with massage or deep massage. Chiropractic adjustment is a beneficial way to maintain a relaxed condition in the spine. The trained practitioner manipulates the spinal column to restore proper functioning of the organs and to maintain balance throughout the body. Through both techniques, one can focus on locked-in tension in parts of the body ruled by the Sun and Saturn. Even more trust and willingness to be vulnerable will be required for the next step—*Rolfing*.

Rolfing, Riechian psychotherapy, and bioenergetic therapy can be very useful in releasing energy blocks. Wilhelm Reich postulated a theory that painful emotions experienced early in life become locked into the muscles of the body. In order to release the emotions, it is necessary to manipulate the *fasciae* (connective tissue) of the muscles. As the Rolfer exerts pressure on parts of the body (pressure that can be quite painful), the emotions stored in the muscles begin to rise to the surface of consciousness where they can be confronted. Reichian psychiatrists and bioenergetic therapists are trained to work on the body and mind together using similar release techniques. While Saturnian people focus on their physical discomfort, the therapist will ask questions. Responses are remarkably truthful; and, because attention has been diverted, the defense mechanisms are much less effective. Once the repressed emotion is unlocked, the patient and therapist can work jointly to resolve the Saturnian feelings of not being "good enough," of emptiness, abandonment and self-condemnation. These feelings, which have been blocking the improvement of self-image, can not be effectively eliminated on the physical level. Many people will be able to work much more successfully with their Saturn internal limitations if they first confront them on the physical plane.

Clearly, those with strong Saturns must have a great deal of trust and confidence in a therapist to try this sort of intense therapy. Usually, this doesn't occur until their late 20's (the Saturn Return) when the emotional pain of unresolved problems is felt very consciously. Between the ages of 28 and 31, there is often an eagerness to tackle some of the long-standing chronic issues which have impeded growth. Therapeutic assistance will be helpful at any time in life if there is a commitment to making it work, but the time of a Saturn Return or transit is especially helpful. People are eager for advancement in their path of development. Yet, when all is said, much depends on their willingness to try. When a person is ready to move, the truth is that almost anything will work. One could sit in the corner and repeat *anything* for five hours a day—it will work if there is a true commitment to change.

MOON/SATURN

The Moon, the fundamental female energy, represents the mother or the woman who provided nurturance. This may have been a woman other than the mother; perhaps, a grandmother, aunt or older sister. Individuals with Moon/Saturn contacts in their birth charts rarely feel emotionally supported by the females in their life, particularly early in their life. Since the Moon represents the soul and Saturn is the Great Teacher, the Moon/Saturn person seems to need to experience this initial lack of nurturance for the soul's growth. The danger is that these people will retreat from developing their own abilities to nurture others; or they will focus the majority of their energies in nurturing others, but will not allow themselves to be nurtured.

Men with Moon/Saturn

Men with Moon/Saturn often are so sensitized to the emotional needs of the mother (needs that appear to them to be excessive) that they frequently take the position of refusing to nurture others. There may also be a deeper level of not trusting nurturing from anyone. As adults they often require a female friend or mate who will provide emotional support without expecting any in return. A crisis occurs when the woman expresses emotional needs that the man interprets as demands. He becomes fearful of the cost to himself or of his inability to give what is asked. Retreat seems the only option. One of the ways out of this trap is, of course, therapy. But, typical of Saturn, he will not trust a therapist unless it becomes clear that maintaining his perspective is more detrimental than taking a chance on trusting another person to help.

Our society does not provide outlets for men to openly express emotion. Therapy, therefore, may be the only option for many—an option that is resisted strongly. If the Moon/Saturn man can develop a mutual emotionally-supportive, non-sexual relationship with an older woman (a few months may be sufficiently older) he can often begin to overcome his intrinsic fear and mistrust of women. Co-workers are often useful in this context. What is important is that there are clearly defined limits to the possibilities in the relationship. This satisfies the Saturnian need for limits, boundaries or structures.

Women with Moon/Saturn

These women frequently choose to be nurturers, appearing to others to be so strong that they need no emotional support themselves. The most important thing a Moon/Saturn woman can do to overcome her isolation is to ask someone for help. It's less frightening to do this in stages and with minor needs; such as, calling a friend and asking to be picked up when you are both going to the same place. Nurturance in American society is frequently expressed through food. So allowing another person to cook for you (not on special occasions) is another important possible first step. The underlying motivation for the "super-nurturer" is often part of a hidden-agenda—to be a better nurturer than mother was. The blame-placing mechanism of Saturn and its ambition to be perfect leads to the Moon/Saturn woman wanting to out-do her mother as a mother or nurturer. As with Sun/Saturn, the Moon/Saturn person feels either unlovable or that he/she must work hard to earn the love and admiration of others.

Another manifestation of Moon/Saturn in women is similar to the mistrust of women that shows up in men. If the woman was raised in a typically traditional family, she will seek friendships with women who are active in the world, rather than with those primarily devoted to their families. But, as she accepts her own femaleness in her late 20's, she may enlarge the circle of her female friends to include these others. If, however, the Moon/Saturn woman was raised in a less rigidly traditional family, she may not differentiate between the lifestyles of women as strongly when choosing her female friends.

The Moon encompasses the emotional life on both the conscious and unconscious levels. Specific emotions are represented by other planets, but the Moon represents the general emotional response to the environment. The Moon is the fastest moving body in the chart, and it ties together all the various levels of the mind. When upset, a person will think with emotional bias, impairing the ability to reason objectively. The integration of the emotional and mental functions is formed during the Lunar phase from birth to age seven. Focus during the child's first seven years should be on the needs of the Moon sign, rather than the Sun and Mercury signs. This is the period in which the major life patterning takes form. Any additional patterning in later life will also refer to the Moon.

A Moon/Saturn contact may point to a mother who is widowed, divorced or must work outside the home for income. Even in cases where both parents are present in the home (and one income is sufficient), the mother may decide to work for reasons of professional growth and career development. As with Sun/Saturn the child feels deserted and unloved by the mother and somehow, responsible for the parent's absence. Many Moon/Saturn people develop "oral fixations" as teenagers or young adults. As infants, these people usually didn't have enough sucking (sucking represents nurturance to an infant.) In the 1920's, 1930's and part of the 1940's it was considered 'modern' by authorities (Saturn) to restrict sucking by limiting how long infants could nurse a bottle or suckle at the breast, or to deny them pacifiers and to pull their thumbs from their mouths. These youngsters are the ones most likely to become smokers and overeaters—often at the first Saturn opposition.

Moon/Saturn people often feel abandoned or intensely disliked by their mothers. With a heavy concentration of Earth/Water they may over-interpret small incidents. An example is an incident in the childhood of a client who had the Moon in Virgo in contact with Saturn in Pisces. This girl was afraid of thunder and lightening. One summer day, when she was about four, she was playing in the backyard when an intense storm suddenly blew up. She ran to the screened-in back door of the house only to find it locked. She cried for her mother to open the door, but her mother was busy in another part of the house. In the few moments that it took for her mother to come and unlock the door, this girl in her terror became convinced that her mother hated her and wished her dead. In recovering this incident during an astrological consultation, the client realized that she had unfairly shut her mother out of her life from that point on. One of her fetishes then became extreme cleanliness, which she remembers using to gain the approval of Mom, a careful housekeeper. When she spoke to her mother about the incident and her feelings surrounding it, her mother, of course, didn't recall such a minor (from her perspective) incident, but she did tell her daughter how she had always loved her. This was the opening to build a new relationship.

Lunar and Saturn Returns

The characteristic quality of a child's relationship to the parent(s) acts as a reference point from which the person forms relationships with other men and women. The Moon/Saturn adult will have carried over into relationships with women those problems inherent in the relationship with the mother. When Moon/Saturn individuals reach their late 20's and experience a progressed Lunar Return and a transiting Saturn Return, they may feel an emptiness in relationships with women and in their own emotional lives; or, they may have no close relationships with women. They are probably still convinced that their mothers didn't love them.

A woman may, for the first time since early youth, establish a close friendship with another woman who is neither a wife nor a mother, but "a person first and a woman second." The Moon/Saturn female prefers to avoid the traditional Saturnian image of women devoted to home and family. Later, as she becomes more trusting and receives some positive emotional feedback, she will be more accepting of traditionally minded women.

During the Lunar and Saturn Returns, men may respond by seeking a woman who will manifest their Lunar energies. They often decide to marry in their late 20's because they feel a lack of feminine energy and need a woman to compensate for this need.

It is a Saturn truism that life can get better as you get older. Some people simply get tired of being miserable; others offer it up as part of their religious or spiritual experience, which can work to ease pain. There are those, too, who "get stuck" in the sorrow of their old disappointments. Certain that they are helpless and that nobody is good enough to help them, they simply withdraw. This is very sad and unnecessary. If you aren't willing to take a chance on living, life is not going to work for you. To live is to be willing to take chances and to risk (something which neither Saturn nor Pluto like). If you are not taking chances then you are "existing" and that's quite a bit different from "living." The answer lies in risking—not letting your Saturn fears, rigidity and early negative assumptions run your life.

MERCURY/SATURN

Youngsters with Mercury/Saturn contacts need to prove to parents, and perhaps to teachers, the validity of their statements and thoughts. They feel, often rightly, that they receive considerable resistance from dominant adults who tell them they're wrong, who won't allow them to speak and, worst of all, who belittle them. However, Mercury/Saturn children are often rescued by one or more teachers who, in the style of true teachers, cherish and promote the children's intellectual growth.

As adults, Mercury/Saturn types are deep thinkers or serious-minded individuals. They are inclined to be scientific, in the true sense, with a need to understand objectively and to examine in detail the functioning of everything in the universe. They investigate the existing order and structure of their environment, have extremely retentive minds, and are proficient at most intellectual pursuits. They do, however, like to learn or study at their own pace. Above all, they need to be "right" and they can be rigid in their attitudes.

Mercury/Saturn types value sincerity and they really believe what they say. It may be difficult for them to express themselves directly, but they never make promises or commitments rashly, and deception is anathema to them. They have either thought about it for a long time or have run it through a checklist of instantaneous criteria that shows them that what they are saying is okay. Mercury/Saturn will not make commitments they cannot fulfill and, once the commitment is made, they will work their fingers to the bone to complete it.

On the negative side, Mercury/Saturn people can be depressive, overly disciplined, with too narrow or too rigid an outlook on life. They are often worriers, constantly rehashing or rethinking previous situations which can lead to feelings of self-reproachment. They're into the "shoulds": "I should have said. . . ." or "I should have handled it. . . ." They are fully able to reconstruct an entire conversation in their minds in elaborate detail, often concluding that their own actions are less than satisfactory. They are also able to write and rehearse fully developed scripts with detailed dialogue before making any communication they consider important. For example, if they're invited to a party, they will spend days creating imaginary conversations: "I will tell George . . . George will say . . . then I will say. . . ." When they finally get to the party, they tell George, but George says something totally different. He didn't get a copy of the script. Mercury/Saturn people are surprised and then have to "wing it" which they do very well once they let go of their fixed ideas.

They should write the first sentence, then get on with life, instead of trying to precondition the entire situation.

It is interesting that Mercury/Saturn people do not like to admit that they worry. They prefer to think of this mentally exhaustive process as "considering all the possibilities." If Neptune is strong in the chart, the possibilities are endless and can be highly imaginative and original. These people need to depersonalize their thinking by directing their mental energies outside themselves. This can be accomplished by reading, taking classes, or going out and having fun, as long as their minds are occupied.

There are several ways to alleviate the "worry mechanism." One can take a mind-control course, which is virtually what the words Mercury and Saturn mean (mind and control). Mind control techniques do not remove conscious awareness (something that is terrifying to Mercury/Saturn types, who can't stand the idea of not knowing what is going on around them). My mother studied Astrology long before I did. She told me that Capricorn, and particularly Mercury in Capricorn (similar to Mercury/Saturn), doesn't like to miss a thing. So they sleep with their eyes partly open when they are children. Since then I have watched children with Mercury in Capricorn take naps with their eyes half open. Mercury/Saturn types don't need to worry about mind control—they will be fully conscious. Mind control, in fact, leads to more responsiveness and less rigidity. An interesting technique from Silva Mind Control is to imagine a blackboard in your mind. On it write a sentence that you are repeatedly rehashing in your mind, one that seems to be relentlessly in your thoughts. You then erase the mental blackboard. This is a wonderful way of eradicating troublesome thoughts that seem to cling to the conscious mind.

Physical movement is another way to dispose of unwanted thought. Simply walk out of a room or current visual impasse. This gives your mind a chance to refocus itself and establish a new perspective. The act of walking into another room while deliberately thinking of something else will do the trick. In fact, any form of travel, whether it is short or long, is a most effective way of changing perspective. When you travel, you leave your troubles at home, and it takes a while for them to catch up with you. Mercury/Saturn symbolizes travel—the motion (Mercury) of separation (Saturn). Trips do not need to be long or expensive. The secret is in changing the visual impact. You could stay overnight with a friend in a different apartment or house. Spending a weekend at a hotel has an amazing effect on a relationship in which Mercury and Saturn are involved, whether in one person's chart or between the two charts.

VENUS/SATURN

In all Venus/Saturn contacts there never seems to be enough love and affection, enough emotional support, or, in reality, enough hugging. What is important with Venus/Saturn is the "feeling" of desertion or abandonment, not necessarily a physical separation, although this may be the case. Since child support and nurturance usually fall on the mother, a Venus/Saturn contact most often involves her.

Separation can occur in any number of ways—the mother may have to care for an ill relative, be hospitalized herself, or the child may be hospitalized. The child may feel a deep sense of desertion. Even though the circumstances surrounding the separation from the mother may be relatively unimportant, the child's reaction will be strong and the event long-remembered. Sometimes this leads to selfishness as Venus/Saturn people seek from others that which was in short supply and often don't give in return. They become convinced that they must "fill the empty space" within and don't even consider that love needs to be a two-way street before that empty space can be filled.

An example of the deep effect a childhood separation can have cropped up in the case of a client whose husband had been having short extra-marital affairs. She interpreted this to mean that he was "shopping" and intended to leave her when he found a suitable replacement. She developed asthma (Venus in an Air sign) and at one point needed to be hospitalized. Her insistence that he would leave her intensified when she was in the hospital. In talking this over, I asked her if, in her childhood, she had been separated from her mother due to illness. She couldn't remember, but since she was planning to visit her parents, I encouraged her to explore this on the chance that her fear of abandonment had its root in such a separation. Upon her return, she reported that when she asked her mother, her mother broke down and cried, explaining that when my client was three years old she needed a tonsillectomy (Saturn in Taurus) and the authorities (Saturn) wouldn't permit her mother to stay with her in the hospital. Awakening at night in a strange place without her mother she became convinced that she had been deserted. The mother carried guilt for not opposing the authorities more successfully. The capper is that it was 30 years later (a Saturn cycle) when this all came out!

People often carry these subconscious memories of separation for years without realizing the power they have to color beliefs and assumptions. The intense feeling of desertion can be reenacted again and again in situations in later years because people believe it has to be this way. Attitude is everything. If people believe on an internal level that they will never be loved, then they never will be. Even if they are capable of receiving love, fear of being abandoned keeps them from letting anyone get close. A Venus/Saturn child who feels unloved pushes the parent even further away. Believing the parent is going to stop showing affection, the child feels it is safer not to give the parent a chance to start. Saturn wants to be in control of the relationship all the time; it will not be made vulnerable. This attitude has long-range ramifications when we deal with Venus/Saturn at an adult level.

A compliment is a form of love and affection, or at least attention, so it follows that Venus/Saturn types have trouble accepting compliments. They often don't hear them and, even more often, forget them. Generally, they view compliments as insincere or self-seeking. Saturn makes Venus feel that affection has to be earned or that there must be a specific reason for the compliment, other than affection. Venus/Saturn people never give compliments they don't mean, but they don't believe other people operate the same way. If you're a Saturn type you'll hear yourself in these interchanges: "What a lovely dress. . . . This old thing." "You gave a terrific presentation last night. . . . Well, thank you, but I've been studying for

a long time." If you do this, then bite your tongue! This is all negative Saturn. Saturn must be able to explain the compliment. Unconditional affection or attention from another person is not acceptable.
The person giving the compliment feels that the Saturn person
doesn't care about his affection or opinion. Ironically, the last thing
Saturn people want is to leave others with the impression that they
don't care about them. So if you're a Venus/Saturn type, learn to
receive those compliments with grace, trust and a smile—even
though you're still saying "Yes, but. . . ." inside. With practice, you'll
begin to feel more comfortable about receiving affection or compliments. It's working from the outside in, changing exterior behavior
first.

Venus/Saturn types usually think they are liked for practical
considerations—dependability, loyalty, their down-to-earth personality; certainly not because they are lovable. It is useful and reward-
ing for Saturn people to ask their friends why they like them (although this may be disconcerting to the friend). At the point of
asking this critical question, Venus/Saturn people have some interesting bodily reactions—upset stomach, knocking knees, headache
and tightened lower back. All the Cardinal sign parts of the body are
communicating a single fear—"this person doesn't really like me."
As would be expected, the friend's response is usually overwhelmingly supportive.

For the child, nurturance in the Lunar sense means sucking
and feeding; in the Venus sense, physical affection. At the beginning
of life, the similar needs of these planets interface. A child who is
fed, but not cuddled at the same time, often has food problems in
adulthood. There may, for instance, be a particular type of food that
seems to supply the affection the child didn't receive in early life. For
people in psychotherapy, these foods are often milk and ice cream.
Ice cream, the great American panacea, is cold (Saturn), made of
milk (Moon) and has lots of sugar (Venus). Guess what's in the
United States chart? Venus in Cancer square Saturn. And what are
ulcers all about? You get to go back and be a baby again, you get to
drink milk. Another Venus/Saturn health problem is overindulgence
in foods with refined sugar and carbohydrates, leading to an imbalance in blood sugar levels.

Hugging and cuddling are both forms of love and affection. Since Venus rules the tactile sensations, Venus/Saturn people are acutely aware of not receiving enough physical affection in their childhood. As adults, they may be very generous in expressing physical affection, thereby ensuring that those they care for will feel loved and wanted. But it is very difficult for them to be the recipient of this type of affection. Women have more opportunity in our society to express physical affection openly. Men usually limit their expression to back slapping and are apprehensive about the more effusive forms. Society views physical affection between men and women almost exclusively in a sexual context, and so it is difficult to express affection comfortably or easily. The Venus/Saturn person must be willing to disregard what other people think—a tough assignment.

But it's on the receiving end of affection that Venus/Saturn types have their real problems. That's because they are still operating from fears of desertion or abandonment. A "reciprocal hug agreement" is recommended. Every time you and a friend get together, you agree to give each other a hug. Sounds simple, but not for the Venus/Saturn person. If you're the Saturn person, select a friend you've known a long time, someone you trust, and explain the exercise (particularly if the friend is of the opposite sex). You'll notice immediately that there is a substantial psychological difference on the receiving end of the hug. Warmth seems to be coming into you from the other person. The next time you meet your friend, you will notice that you are now in a vulnerable position— you have to wait for the other person to initiate a hug. And during this waiting period (although only a few moments) you will experience all those Cardinal point tensions in the stomach, head, knees and back. Then, suddenly, the friend moves toward you—the hug happens. Sometimes, this is the first time in years that the Saturn person has allowed someone to give affection without any special "reason." As you gain confidence, hugging becomes easier to apply in all relationships.

Venus/Saturn in Love Relationships

Venus/Saturn people often confuse love and sexuality. One way to receive love and affection they have learned, is in a sexual situation.

But, as they begin to differentiate between the need for affection (Venus) and sexual expression (Mars), they may encounter periods of loss of sexual drive. What is happening is that energies, previously channeled almost exclusively in sexual expression, are now being focused on self-improvement, on internal "repair" after emotionally unsatisfying relationships. As they withdraw from sexual activity, they learn to deal with their needs for nonsexual affection, as represented by Venus. When they can distinguish clearly between love and sex, they often realize that the Venus need is much stronger than the sexual need. Interestingly, Venus precedes Earth, and Mars follows in orbits outward from the Sun. Venusian needs must be met first before we can function fully on the sexual level of Mars.

As in other relationships, Venus/Saturn types find it hard to believe their mates can love them for other than good practical reasons. A man, for example, will think of himself as a good provider and communicate his love this way. Venus/Saturn people tend to measure love in terms of material value (Saturn rules the material plane). They instinctively know what a gift costs and will measure the person's love according to the price of the gift versus the ability to give. Venus/Saturn individuals also measure love in terms of "time" (Saturn): "How much time do they spend with me?" They tend to feel jealous of anyone their mates spend time with, then dip into sadness, loneliness and self-pity: "I don't deserve love. . . ." "No one could love me." These people need to learn to verbalize their needs, and to take the chance that their mates or lovers do love them. Any serious romance that fizzled in the late teens or through age 20 (the Venus period) may stamp Venus/Saturn types with a deeper belief of their being unlovable. One must thoroughly process such an early disappointment.

If people are put off by Venus/Saturn types it may be because they are unwilling to expose their shortcomings and fears. They mask their lack of self-esteem, fear of making mistakes and uncertainty about their future with a confident, "in-charge" exterior. A diminished sense of self-worth can also take a nasty turn: "I'm not worth much, so anyone who loves me must not be worth much, either." Venus/Saturn people begin to treat their partners this way and will need to break through the judgment of their own unworthiness in order to stop projecting this view onto their partner.

Couples with Venus/Saturn contacts (in individual charts or between charts) often negotiate time contracts, committing themselves to spending time together. If one person breaks the contract, the other deprives the partner of something important. A wife may stop cooking her husband's favorite foods; a husband won't take his wife to her favorite places. The most powerful weapon in the arsenal of both partners is, of course, the withholding of sexual expression. But, behind all these games is the need to love and be loved.

An inversion of the 'time contract' is another Venus/Saturn game called 'less is more'. In this game the person will enter a relationship, then decide not to see the other person. Venus and Saturn are saying: "I am going to spend less and less time with you and see if you will still be there. You can prove your love for me by allowing me not to give you what you need, yet be there for me. If you stay, thereby proving your love for me, maybe I'll let you come closer." This destructive dynamic usually occurs because the Venus/Saturn person has been severely hurt in love relationships, family life or friendships. The other person will need patience and understanding to meet this Saturnian test of their relationship, a test usually lasting for two and a half to three years, the time it takes Saturn to transit a sign.

Early in relationships, Venus/Saturn people exhibit fear of vulnerability and commitment. This usually takes the form of not admitting tender feelings for the other person. Sometimes they will after the other person does so first (this can be a real bind when both people have Venus/Saturn). Once a relationship is established a Venus/Saturn person will often withdraw or end it because of fear that the other person is going to do this, and the need to avoid being hurt again. If the fear of commitment is very great, the Venus/Saturn person won't let a relationship develop fully—wanting only a casual, sexual and social connection. This allows the individual to stay in control, but it also guarantees emptiness. The offices of therapists and marriage counselors throng with those who have not been taught to express love, but who have mastered avoidance.

MARS/SATURN

Mars is your energy; Saturn limits, restricts, or controls. What you get with contact between these two planets is repressed anger— actually fear/anger (Saturn/Mars). People with these contacts often turn their anger into fear or their fear into anger and it all implodes. Let's see how this works at various levels.

The most frequent effect of Mars/Saturn is a blocking of the drives to initiate action and sexuality, except in those moments when the fire of Mars melts the repressive hand of Saturn and you get extreme expression of Martian characteristics. In childhood, Mars/Saturn youngsters are usually discouraged, sometimes directly disciplined, for expressing anger. They interpret this: "If you want approval, don't be rambunctious, don't express yourself fully, hold back." Thus begins the withholding of the easy flow of Martian energies. On the physical level, these children usually turn to highly-disciplined team sports or other forms of channeled physical energy such as gymnastics or ballet. In their teens, they may go all out for 'contact' sports, or, convinced of the wrongness of violence, seek to channel their energy into hypersexuality. Hypersexuality is the mechanism by which they can calm fears that their sexual energy will run out or not be fully expressed. Highly athletic people use up most of their Martian energy in athletics. Non-athletic types are often more active sexually.

Women with Mars/Saturn often struggle with unresolved in- cestuous feelings toward their fathers, well into adult life. This oc- curs when as physically-developing teenagers the father (Saturn) withdraws his attention because he is uncomfortable with his daugh- ter's sexuality (Mars). She is no longer "Daddy's little girl" and feels deserted. Although she may not consciously connect the withdrawal to her developing sexuality, nevertheless she goes into adult life punishing (Saturn) herself, either by low orgasmic potential or by not finding a suitable mate.

Some Mars/Saturn people are convinced that their anger (sup- pressed energy) can become lethal; even minor instances of phys- ical threat can reinforce this fear. In this century, with the increase of violence in war, civil disorder, TV and films, many Mars/Saturn children have become paranoid with the fear of being hurt or of hurting others. In defense and to convince themselves they are not weak, these people are often bullying or bossy in childhood, fighting or belittling others in adulthood. If Mars/Saturn children have experienced actual violence to themselves or in their environment, they may feel that physical violence is normal. If they can talk about these experiences as adults (which they rarely do), they can often see the abnormality of the situation. The double-edged sword here is that guilt at having needed punishment may be transmuted into rage at themselves and others. Saturn needs to fix blame—so they may justify their parents' violence toward them as necessary, deserved punishment. Extreme examples of this occur in child-abuse cases. Some of these parents will even ask, "Why did you make me lose my temper and hurt you?" This convinces the children that they are responsible, even to the point that they can control negative behavior in others. As adults, they feel that it is their fault that they attract physical abuse or rejection. Metaphysically, they are choosing only those people or situations that will manifest in these occurrences and thus repeat the familiar pattern.

Mars/Saturn energy can work in two directions—toward failure or toward the focused energy that creates success. In the failure mode, the timing factor of Saturn leads these people to underestimate the time or energy required to complete a task. When they recognize this failure in judgment, they will often simply stop, give up. Also involved in this scenario is a fear of not being capable of accomplishing what they have committed themselves to accomplish. This underestimating of time and energy required becomes a built-in safety valve, an excuse for not succeeding. In a working situation, this behavior generates anger from those who must cope with the Mars/Saturn person's unwillingness to take full responsibility and to gauge time and energy realistically. Naturally, alienation only reinforces the Mars/Saturn script, "I'm no good." Once in a while, you run into people who simply won't accept any responsibility, usually because when they were younger, they didn't get what they wanted from some commitment.

Here's an example of a man whose Sun/Saturn conjunction in Gemini opposed Mars in Sagittarius. When he was a child, the boy and his father worked around the house together. Just before the father left town for a brief trip, he gave the boy a job to do—one which the boy, of course, carried out to perfection. When the father returned, his son was eager for his appreciation. The father, however, was busy and didn't get around to looking at the work for three days. Then all he said was, "It's O.K." That did it! The boy didn't get the response he felt was due him. As an adult, he was fired from numerous jobs—all of them for not completing his work. Some Mars/Saturn people, obviously, use the positive potential in this aspect—focused, exacting use of energy to complete tasks no matter how much time and energy is required.

In those who accept responsibility (Saturn) for their own actions (Mars), this contact produces a determined thrust to complete any task on time and perfectly. Their need to live up to these standards can even produce the "workaholic" type. Tense or tight muscles are only the first hint of the stress that too great a perfectionism places on these people.

In its best manifestation, this contact is seen in those people who love their work, can balance it with fun, and who get even more energetic when there are difficult circumstances to conquer.

All Mars/Saturn contacts need body work to release the internal tension set up by either syndrome—failure or dogged determination to complete a task perfectly. If they don't learn how to externalize negative feelings, illness can result. Although most people are not conscious of the process, internalized negativity gradually begins to affect the physical vehicle. The nature and characteristics of the disease usually correlate with the emotional and astrological patterns. Health professionals are only now beginning to make breakthroughs in their investigations of the effect of emotions on the body.

Mars/Saturn people usually have a rigid musculature, one that needs to be loosened. Saturn acts to control and clutch the muscles. Many of the physical therapeutic techniques described earlier with Sun/Saturn contacts are also useful with Mars/Saturn. Rigorous exercise, because of its muscle contraction, only reinforces rigidity; while physical activities such as swimming, dancing and yoga promote movement that is rhythmic and flowing. These people should also consider deep massage once a week or at other frequent intervals when physical stress is evident. Rolfing is also indicated; but, as explained earlier, this person must be willing to accept the physical discomfort of the treatment. Usually, Saturnian pain works in a positive way since Mars/Saturn people believe nothing is of any lasting value unless some degree of pain is present. Any method promoting more flexibility in the body will help the person to externalize or reduce anger in a positive way. As this occurs, progress on the internal level will become apparent.

JUPITER/SATURN

Children with these contacts are very sensitive to the impact of their behavior on those around them and they consider rightness and fairness very important. If disciplinary actions (Saturn) taken by others are unfair, they can be outraged. But as Jupiter/Saturn children mature, they recognize the value of personal restraint for the sake of social continuity. Jupiter/Saturn types are concerned with their immediate environment, the neighborhood in which they live or work, and the people with whom they have daily contact. It is the outer planets (Uranus, Neptune and Pluto) that focus on the impersonal, collective social structure.

When Jupiter/Saturn children feel comfortable in their environment they often exhibit the bubbly enthusiasm of Jupiter. However, when harshly called to task, this may change quickly to shyness or negativism. If an adult says, "Settle down, you're getting out of hand," this implies that "people in general" won't find their behavior acceptable, not just parents and other adults. Then Jupiter/Saturn children fold in on themselves, extinguishing their lively light. As adults, the real task of Jupiter/Saturn individuals is to let their light show consistently, whether it is "socially acceptable" or not. They need to associate with others who are alive and vital, not with joy-killers.

Jupiter/Saturn Phases

The phase of your birth Jupiter/Saturn can disclose your position in a reincarnation cycle. Those born from the conjunction to the opening square are in the beginning of a new series of lives. Here the emphasis is on gathering as much life experience as possible. The first half of the Jupiter/Saturn cycle is primarily Jupiter energy, so little conscious thought is given to correcting the mistakes of the past.

People born with Jupiter and Saturn between the opening square and the opposition are still very involved with collecting experience, but they have become more structured, more selective as to the type of experience. They may, for instance, give more focus to business or home life.

Those born with Jupiter/Saturn from the opposition to the closing square are now shifting gears, becoming more concerned with working with the accumulated experience rather than gathering new experience. They are more concerned with trying to do the right thing in every area of life.

The Jupiter/Saturn phase from the closing square until the next conjunction is, in my opinion, what Marc Jones called "the last chance lifetime." It may be one of the last in a series of lives, so consciousness is focused on correcting the mistakes of the past (karma) in very specific areas, such as business, family, etc. If Saturn is angular in any Jupiter/Saturn phase, there is a sense of not having much time left. In the final phase, this sense pervades the lifetime.

Because people with Saturn in contact with Jupiter have a well developed moral structure and tend toward rigid idealism, it is important for them to be raised in religions of love, not those that emphasize fear and guilt (Saturn). The trouble is that most Western religions have emphasized the Saturn qualities. Even if Jupiter/Saturn people cease to practice their religion, the acquired fear and guilt have long-term implications. Jupiter is attracted to pleasure and the comfortable life, while Saturn makes the person feel guilty and unworthy. Those with rigid religious upbringing feel guilty for allowing themselves to enjoy happiness and success. They may even underplay and hide achievements for fear of being viewed as selfish or self-absorbed. When it comes to money, Jupiter/Saturn individuals may be secretive about the amount they possess. They don't use money ostentatiously. They fear others will think they are materialistic. (Jupiter/Saturn can also indicate weight problems.) If, however, they haven't been raised to associate fear and guilt with religion, they will enjoy the good things life has to offer without guilt. Even if they receive negative feedback on their financial and professional successes, they won't be disturbed. They know they have earned their success. People with positive religious or moral indoctrination know there is nothing wrong with having money or visible signs of physical comfort. They can feel good about a big house, fancy car or expensive clothing. Money is a commodity, there for the benefit of everyone, and these people are able to give it freely to friends, family members, or charitable institutions. The Saturn type can only come to these perspectives later in life as "rewards" for their hard work.

When people have had primarily happy experiences in their religious or moral training, they will be generous with themselves and others (Jupiter expands). Conversely, if their moral or religious experiences were unhappy, they will handle money in a miserly, guilty fashion (Saturn contracts).

When the Jupiter/Saturn contact is also associated with personal planets and points there is often a swing in moods or mental perspective between the highs (Jupiter) and the lows (Saturn). The body will also respond to this combination by either an extreme of Jupiter (overweight) or of Saturn (too thin). Only in cases where many personal points or plants are involved along with other outer planets will you sometimes see the state that psychiatry refers to as manic/depressive.

SATURN/URANUS

Saturn wants to keep everything within bounds, in check. Uranus refuses to admit that there are any boundaries (implying, of course, that there are). People with Saturn/Uranus contacts in their birth chart see-saw between playing it safe (Saturn) and taking spontaneous chances (Uranus). The result is a conflict between freedom and security, free-wheeling and self-control, trying to maintain position and security while still wanting to do their own thing.

Note which of these two planets is earlier in zodiacal longitude. If Saturn comes first, then the natural flow of planetary energy outward from the Sun is maintained, and the person seeks to build security. The problem is that fear (Saturn) can cause the individual to become locked into this position, seeking more and more security. At the time of its transit to Saturn, Uranus energy can then be used to break the crystallization and make way for new ideas or experiences. But when Uranus appears first in the zodiac the energy works in reverse. Rebellion (Uranus) becomes crystallized (Saturn) when Saturn by transit contacts the Uranus position. The person may then become locked into rebellion against society. These individuals find it very hard to give up their revolutionary ideas. Others with Uranus first in the zodiac, don't go through teenage rebellion completely. In the midlife crisis (when both Saturn and Uranus aspect their own natal positions), the see-saw effect of the planets reaches a climax and, for the first time, they have a chance to break through their own self-imposed reactionary attitudes. The positive side of having Uranus earlier in the zodiac and Saturn second is that it allows the person to formalize, solidify and sometimes ritualize positive changes.

All this on-again, off-again quality of Saturn/Uranus can create tension that is very hard to deal with. It means you must apply caution when you don't want to, move ahead when you're afraid to, in order to use the energy positively.

In childhood, the message from the adult world is "Be original, but don't go too far," or, "Don't be original at all." The implication is that there is something either wrong or dangerous in not conforming. In the latter case, you will need much intense inner work to develop your creativity. In the first instance, it may be easier to take chances with self-expression. Encouragement from friends or beloved teachers is often the only impetus needed.

But Uranus energy is not ultimately controllable, so Saturn/Uranus individuals must eventually learn that their only "security" is in their uniqueness, in their willingness to "march to the tune of a different drummer." The highest expression of Saturn/Uranus is the ability to take forms of the past that have proven viable (Saturn) and combine them with new insights that will move the person confidently and productively into the future (Uranus).

SATURN/NEPTUNE

This is the prime metaphysical indicator of the "initiate." Saturn rules the material plane, symbolized by the physicality of earth and our bodies. In this plane, our senses assure us that material structures are "real". But Neptune, planet of the spiritual, the intangible, recognizes no structures, no boundaries. It dissolves them to obtain a more inclusive view. Surprisingly, Western thought now seems to reinforce these seemingly antithetical Saturn and Neptune perspectives. Modern physics is showing us, through scientific method, what Eastern mystics have long taught. Material existence is actually brought about by intangible energy not recognized by the five senses. While Saturn appears to be real because it is tangible, Neptune seems unreal in its intangibility. Yet, it is how we think that conditions the world—this is the lesson to be ultimately grasped through Saturn/Neptune contacts. What appears to be real is actually in a state of becoming. It is intangible, spiritual energy that determines which way the flux will appear in the next instant.

Saturn/Neptune children are often aware of the disparity between their perception of truth, beauty and idealism, and the reality of the society in which they live. They may not have the intellectual equipment to state this in these terms, but they do sense that what they feel most comfortable with is either unrecognized, discounted, or disparaged by the people around them. If these children have creative abilities that are recognized and encouraged by others, they may escape the worst sense of unhappiness this contact implies. But, often, their creative abilities are sacrificed to the practicalities of daily life.

Saturn/Neptune adults, motivated by their own sorrow at being disconnected from their inner sense of truth, often delve into spiritual or metaphysical systems seeking answers thus allowing them to become "initiates." In its most negative form, Saturn/Neptune indicates retreat into drugs, alcohol, or cults to soften the blows that life inflicts daily. If Saturn/Neptune personalities are too fearful of exploring their own inner space, they may displace the energy and become fanatic "do-gooders", constantly finding fault with society.

Disappointment with reality (Saturn) not matching their inner vision (Neptune) can be so pervasive that little in life holds promise of joy, light or love. When this happens they can often save themselves by becoming involved with religious, social or spiritual organizations that have a stated higher purpose. For example, they may do volunteer work to help those less fortunate than themselves or participate in organizations dedicated to the improvement of life on the planet. The main point is to dedicate themselves to something larger than the petty concerns of the Saturn-contained ego; and, to allow the inspiring energies of Neptune to pervade some areas of their lives. In physical terms, the opposing energies of Saturn/Neptune mainfest as the "illness axis" because Neptune erodes or dissolves the material structures of Saturn. When these planets contact personal planets or points, there is the likelihood of constant physical, mental or emotional distress. In order to strengthen their health, these people must find a joyful, inspirational, yet practical philosophy. Their problem will be that most organized Western religions do not emphasize joy—only suffering, which reinforces the negative Saturn/Neptune. They may believe that suffering is "good", having selected such ideas from their upbringing.

SATURN/PLUTO

Saturn and Pluto represent the potential energy needed for growth, development, transformation and the ultimate destruction of that which is no longer needed. This is why Saturn/Pluto contacts are found in the charts of people who are constantly faced with separation from all that is most dear to them. It is their "theme" to accept these tragedies as necessary in order to fulfill a place (however unconscious) in the evolution of their society. Mental acceptance is a vitally important step in transcending the heartwrenching sorrow this contact often promises. Only when the Saturn/Pluto contact is involved with personal points or planets will this be an obvious part of an individual's personal life. Otherwise, it describes a social process of releasing pieces of the collective consciousness for restructuring, such as hateful or destructive energy, prior to a major step in the evolution of human consciousness.

The first major Saturn/Pluto contact, following the discovery of Pluto, occurred during the early 1930's and heralded the rise of Hitler and the European Holocaust of World War II. This negative energy is still resonant in our consciousness because we have not yet accepted our capacity to perpetuate or condone the wholesale horror that is the threat of nuclear holocaust. Only when, collectively, we can grow beyond this dehumanizing position and restructure this low energy can we move up in the spiral of human evolution.

On an individual level, Saturn/Pluto contacts indicate control and power and individuals who can operate easily within power structures. At their highest functioning, these people can contribute their own energies to the life-sustaining objectives of an organization without becoming possessive or compulsive. But those who can't separate their identity from organizations will inevitably begin to play those corporate and political games of over-control and be-hind-the-scenes power-plays that poison the soul.

In personal relationships, Saturn/Pluto individuals want to con-trol absolutely. They often suppress their partners' full expression of needs and desires. Some may select partners who can't express their deepest feelings. Or, if they've chosen mates who can, they may find fault with the content or context of the others' feelings. The obsessive need for control may really point to people who, at heart, want to be conscious of the soul connection with their mate, who cannot let go until this is accomplished or until the relationship has been destroyed. They try to control, then forcibly resist, any change in others that threatens their security. This may extend to not letting relationships end when they should. This compulsive holding-on often is fueled by a larger unconscious life-and-death struggle against the inevitable decay cycles inherent in all life processes and experiences. Once this is seen and accepted, the Saturn/Pluto per-son can participate, through the events of his life, in the necessary collective restructuring implied in world events at the time of his birth and throughout life.

Magic is also the natural province of Saturn/Pluto. The contact is the metaphysical indicator of the "adept". Control of the environ-ment or the self is the goal; control of others is the negative tempta-tion. Today there are many possibilities to connect consciously with the magical, alchemical power of restructured consciousness (Sat-urn/Pluto). Usually these opportunities come through learning (Sat-urn) within "special interest groups" (Pluto) such as consciousness-raising groups, group therapy, *est* training and other such experi-ences. The learning of Saturn can best combine with the catalytic energy of Pluto in such situations. Typically, there is much initial long-lasting resistance in both society and in those with Saturn/Pluto contacts in trying out these or similar remedies.

CHAPTER 3

URANUS

Uranus is the planet of rapid change, sudden insight, freedom, re-bellion, individuality, autonomy, innovation, eccentricity, bi-zarreness, uniqueness and independence. In orbit, it is the first planet beyond Saturn—the first of the "outer" planets, the planets of cosmic awareness. Dane Rudhyar explains this idea beautifully. Saturn, the last planet that can be seen with the naked eye, rules the skin of the solar system, that which we can physically perceive, the material plane. If we have successfully met the demands of Saturn and have learned the lessons of the material plane, then we can travel beyond the limitations of Saturn and experience positive inter-action with Uranus. But we cannot get beyond Saturn by denying its existence. In its revolutionary role, Uranus breaks through the estab-lished, perhaps over-crystallized structure of Saturn, reaching to-ward a more impersonal collective cosmic consciousness. Uranus moves beyond personal identification with the ego toward a broader universal reality. On a personal level, people with a prominent Ura-nus in their birth charts feel different, perhaps alienated, non-con-formist, sometimes disassociated from everything around them—feelings that are difficult to handle psychologically. This feeling of

separation is distinctly different from the Saturnian sense of separation. Saturnian people feel alone because others don't seem to
share the same problems. When they realize others do have the
same types of problems, dilemmas and crises, they are relieved and
begin to feel an interconnectedness with humanity. Uranus individuals, on the other hand, are eternally convinced that they are
unique, different from the rest of humanity; and, they have a big
investment in proving and maintaining this (something they are
often unwilling to admit). As children, they may, for instance, have a
fantasy that they are from another planet, in the sense of having
special powers a step above other humans, but definitely human—
sort of a Superman or Wonderwoman. Or, they may fantasize that
they are misplaced in time, a visitor from the future. They believe,
no single person on the face of the planet can possibly understand
their special "uniqueness". As adults, they feel they have unique
problems and relationships and an identity that is unprecedented.
Uranus types are not interested in fusing their individuality with
other people or with blending into society and conforming to the
strictures of their culture. Although they share identical problems
with others, they will reject the validity for themselves of any advice
that works for others. "That may work for everyone else, but it
won't work for me," is their usual response, illustrating their determination to maintain an individualistic attitude of separateness from
the rest of society. Often extreme emotional pain or discomfort is a
necessary experience before they will allow themselves to join some
of the rest of us and benefit from advice and procedures that work
for others.

An interesting corollary to this idea of "singleness" is observed
in Uranian persons who consistently complain about not being married or involved in a love relationship. Sometimes they lament this
state of singleness all the way into middle-age or old-age without
recognizing the truth about themselves—they don't actually want to
be married or involved in a relationship. Uranians who are married
or in a relationship may also want to be single, which is difficult to
accomplish! This unwillingness to admit the truth applies to all life
situations. Uranians unvolved in any unpleasant situation should
carefully examine the reality present. If they are staying in any unpleasant or unproductive situation after repeatedly struggling with it,
then there is some "payoff" for them. Perhaps the payoff is being

able to complain about their unfortunate circumstances to others, thus gaining attention. Uranians need to develop a conscious awareness of their "true" needs, and then ensure that life situations are compatible with these needs. Most current social attitudes are antithetical to the Uranian need for freedom, thus the importance of knowing oneself well. For instance, there is nothing wrong with living alone, without a mate, even though social programming says otherwise.

Uranus energy often seeks freedom beyond all boundaries. But genuine freedom implies an equal amount of responsibility. In deference to planetary protocol, Saturn precedes Uranus and will confer genuine freedom only after a person has accepted the responsibility ascribed to it. The polar opposite of responsibility is unbridled willfulness. In early life (even into the 40's), this may be expressed as a wanton or reckless drive for freedom with complete disregard for the rights of others. The pejorative side of Uranus seeks to avenge itself in a rebellious way, all in the guise of freedom. These individuals first need to recognize how they are really expressing their drive for freedom. Then they should seek the meaning of true freedom and try to understand their previous concepts concerning it. Pure freedom is possible only when we responsibly consider other people and situations.

Uranians really need "permission" to be different from those close to them. If people around them accept their differences and value their individuality, then Uranians cease to rebel, to parade their freedom. This acceptance must be sincere, however, since Uranians are highly intuitive and will know if it is an empty gesture.

Uranus indicates the sudden reversal of ideas and circumstances. People with a prominent Uranus often change their minds at the last minute and decide to do something opposite to their initial intention. This change is rarely conscious, even when Mercury is involved. Uranus is reliable only in its unexpectedness, its changeability. If everything points in one direction, Uranus will, inevitably, choose the other. If you zig, it will zag.

Before discussing the interaction of Uranus with other planets, I would like to propose an idea concerning sign rulership. According to the Uranian system of Astrology, Uranus is the ruler of Sagittarius. There is definitely some merit to this association, even though there is a strong relationship between Uranus and Aquarius. Sagittarians are often considered unconventional, rebellious, not overly concerned with others' opinions of them. They can be quite frank, candid and outspoken—qualities which don't sit comfortably with Jupiter, the traditional ruler of Sagittarius, which prefers interaction to be pleasant and easy. Uranus is also the higher octave of Mercury, ruler of Gemini and the sign opposing Sagittarius. This postulates a further connection or affinity between Uranus and Sagittarius. When looking at individual charts, then, it is valid to use Uranus as ruler and Jupiter as co-ruler of both Sagittarian and Aquarian houses. This rulership warrants serious investigation and should produce some interesting insights into the birth chart.

In its most positive expression, the strongly Uranian type brings sparkle, verve and zing into the lives of those they contact. Their unusual, even brilliant, perspectives about life or particular issues allow others to consider or follow a new track. In casual social situations, they add fizz to otherwise bland mixtures. They have high auric energy and are usually willing to share it by participating in whatever is going on, rather than by just observing.

SUN/URANUS

A Sun/Uranus contact in the birth chart indicates extreme physical excitability and hyperactivity. The nervous system is high-strung and charged with intense electrical energy (comparable to Sun/Mars contacts, although not as low-key or as constant) that is subject to spasmodic, intermittent fluctuations. Because this strong energy won't allow them to sit still for long, Uranians often jiggle their legs from the hip (Sagittarius) when they sit, or they move about or pace. This is also true of Mars/Uranus and Sun/Mars. The actual energy level is not low, but the basic physical vitality undulates in a somewhat unpredictable pattern of continual ascent and decline.

Another reason to support the affinity of Uranus and Sagittarius is that Uranus, as the planet of change, correlates well with the mutable on-again/off-again quality of Sagittarius. Energy in Aquarius, a fixed sign, has a less tenuous pattern, oscillating in a sudden on/off manner, but at a lower frequency than in mutable Sagittarius.

It is important to understand that this fluctuation of energy is not in the conscious control of the individual, but is modulated by the erratic behavior of the nervous system in response to Uranus. The series of abrupt reversals is a Uranian characteristic. Uranus always seeks to establish a situation diametrically opposed to the existing one. Through attempts to be different or original, Sun/Uranus people continually reverse their stand, usually when even *they* least expect it.

This fluctuating Uranian energy also has medical implications. It can reverse the expected manifestation of certain drugs, medical or conventional techniques. For this reason, Sun/Uranus people should always use extreme caution when selecting a doctor or submitting to any form of treatment. Unusual sleep patterns may be another result of Sun/Uranus contacts. The intermittent action of Uranus can interrupt the sleep cycle at various intervals throughout the night. Entitled *the awakener*, Uranus may literally wake a person every few hours due to the irregular energy flow. (This differs from the Saturn, sometimes Neptune, effect of not being able to fall asleep, or waking up and not falling back to sleep, because of deep-level depression or anxiety). For Uranian individuals, it may be helpful to take time with an activity that can siphon off some of the energy. This allows the body to return to a relaxed state conducive to sleep. Some imaginative channeling of energy to heal the earth not only reduces the person's tension, but satisfies the Uranian's broader social scope.

An elevated state of hypertension can, of course, wear down the body's vitality. The relentless confrontation with internal tension forces the body to function in a condition of stress, and can create a variety of circulatory or heart problems. Sun/Uranus people should find ways to drain off or release this tension. Daily exercise is one of the techniques that can be used, although Sun/Uranus people become quickly bored with any single exercise method. To channel energy successfully, their program should include a wide spectrum of physical activities. Since Uranians pride themselves on being unique, they benefit most from a personally designed program to meet their own specific requirements. Rigorous exercise is particularly useful, since Uranian energy doesn't easily lend itself to low-key, overly structured activities. Uranus prefers activity that is both fast-paced and exciting, such as competitive sports. The iconoclastic nature of Uranus can also point to activities that can be

performed independently—jogging, bicycle riding—or anything of
an adventurous nature—mountain climbing, sky diving, wind sailing
or spelunking. Not contemplative by nature, Sun/Uranus people
find it extremely difficult to relax or meditate unless they have first
eliminated the excess electrical-physical energy. Even then "moving
meditations" such as Yoga, Tai C'hi and Aikido are most suitable for
the Sun/Uranus nervous system.

This "wired" nervous system is sometimes so extreme that in
addition to not being able to sit still, they have difficulty sleeping
very long in ordinary circumstances, but drop off like babies in
airplanes, cars, trains or other moving vehicles. In a way Sun/Ura-
nus people suffer jet lag by being on the planet!

One Sun/Uranus client arrived at work every Monday "ready
to kill." "I can't take it," she announced, "and neither can the
people around me." She had been exercising every day of the
week—except Sunday. I suggested she add this to her schedule,
and it worked.

Sun/Uranus individuals generally expect the men in their lives
to be undependable and unreliable. This is true for charts of men
and women, since the Sun refers to men in the biological sense.
Because Uranians consider themselves unconventional and are
easily bored by men who are ordinary or traditional, their "radar"
will lead them to seek out relationships with only those men who are
somewhat unique and different. The terms unique, different, conventional and traditional are, of course, all relative to an individual's
social reference and conditioning. Each person has biases concerning what is original (as opposed to traditional), and two strongly
Uranian individuals may disagree completely as to the meaning of
these terms. The hightest priority for Uranians is to be different from
everyone else—including other Uranian people. In a very
provocative way, this can become a contest of individuality. People
who personify uniqueness and individuality are those who inevitably surprise and, sometimes, shock and disorient us, and whose
behavior is almost always the opposite of our expectations.

Women with Sun/Uranus will, inevitably, seek men who are
extraordinary and highly individual. If they haven't rebelled enough
in their teen years, when it was appropriate, they will unconsciously
choose lovers or mates whom they know their parents won't like.

Even though Sun/Uranus will choose those who are different, *how* different is a measure of how well the energy has been integrated! If Water/Earth is also strong in their charts, they will experience an inner conflict of needs in relationships with men. Water/Earth seeks secure, predictable relationships built on traditional values, while Uranus seeks the opposite. Women with these conflicts will continually fail to manifest fulfilling relationships because one part of them desires stability, while the other part seeks the freedom and excitement of Uranus. These two relationship expectations are obviously mutually exclusive. First they need to be recognized, and then combined, if possible, in a highly original relationship with a partner who reflects and fulfills both needs. One way to combine stability and freedom is to build "separateness" into a relationship. Both partners need to retain a certain degree of independence. By planning some separate social activities, each has equal freedom, and the needs of both people can be satisfied. Travel by one partner for business reasons can also create freedom for both partners and prevent boredom. Women with Sun/Urananus contacts are so freedom-oriented that they usually choose men who are amenable to the idea of separation. These women don't want to merge themselves in a relationship to the exclusion of everything else.

Although very freedom-conscious for themselves, Sun/Uranus individuals may not feel their partners deserve the same degree of freedom. If the relationship is to work, people with a good deal of freedom through travel or social interaction must be willing to extend these same privileges in parity to their partners.

A woman with Sun/Uranus contacts who selects direct and independent men may have cause to regret the choice later when she begins to perceive the partner as undependable, unreliable, and never around. Gradually, she comes to resent her partner's independence as well as the loss of her own freedom. In a very real sense, her own desires are mirrored in the behavior of the partner. Such women have projected their own real need for freedom and self-assertivenss onto their partners (although they will rarely admit this to themselves). They must begin to reclaim their own Sun/Uranus energy, rather than seek its expression through the partner. Once they are able to express this energy, Uranus women won't feel they're the target of someone else's expression of freedom.

Here's an example of Uranian reversal and its solution. One of my clients, with a Sun in 10th House Aries conjunct Uranus, was married to a man with a 12th House Pisces Sun and a 6th House Virgo Moon. The husband was a successful lawyer who could well afford to pay a housekeeper, but he preferred that his wife do the cooking and cleaning. He would come home every day and run his fingers over the furniture, looking for dust. Though she had never explored the possibility, the wife and a secret yearning to do some sort of work in the world. Six months after I first saw the wife, the husband called for an appointment. His wife had walked out on him (transiting Uranus opposing her natal Sun) and left him the tapes of our sessions. Here was Uranian reversal. She had the 10th House Sun and stayed at home cleaning and cooking. He had a 12th House Sun and 6th House Moon and whenever he came home, he ran his fingers over things. She had picked a man who was active in the world (where she wanted to be), and he insisted his wife express his Virgo Moon energy. I asked him if he wanted to save his marriage. He said, "Yes." I suggested first, that he let his wife do some volunteer work with an organization that was important in the world. Second, that he hire a housekeeper; and, third, that he take specialty cooking lessons, a natural for Virgo. She began volunteer work in a hospital, and within three months was heading a program for liaison between hospital personnel and patients. Eventually she travelled around the country setting up similar programs in other hospitals. The husband went to French cooking school. They entertain a lot, and he often does the cooking. They didn't need to end the marriage; they built originality, freedom and self-expression into it, in terms of their conditioning and background.

If Sun/Uranus individuals have a preponderance of Earth and/or Water in their charts, their security needs are strong. Similar to strong Uranus and Saturn, they want freedom, but also need security. At times, they will be involved in relationships that don't address both needs, yet they remain in them out of convenience or practical considerations. The partner may not be able to live separately due to circumstances, or they may not want to maintain separate social lives all the time. Ultimately, however, the romance ends and may be transformed into either a brother-sister relationship or a marriage. A possible unconscious reason for maintaining a non-sexual arrangement is that (to the couple) the relationship still qualifies as different and unusual. To continue to fight for freedom is tiring. Frequently, as time passes, there is less inclination to be out-wardly different, and the realization that the true Uranian freedom is within oneself.

The Sun/Uranus Father in the Birth Chart

The father of Sun/Uranus individuals doesn't always fit accepted astrological concepts. Although he is often unusual in relation to the world, his personality at home may not be perceived as different from other fathers. He is likely to promote the child's independence, originality and eccentricities, something the child doesn't recognize as unusual until he becomes an adult. Then, if other men do not support the Uranian's independence and originality, as the father did, the Uranian feels short-changed. It is not unusual for the father to come from a different cultural background than that experienced by the child. Often he is an immigrant or first-generation American. The father's work may also be typical of Uranus—scientific, engi-neering, electronics, computer science. Although the father's work may create sporadic contact with the child, the child will not see this as abandonment, but rather as a lack of dependability. The father may also make contradictory statements—at one moment encour-aging the child's individuality, then strongly stating the reverse. This Uranian quality of sudden reversals and extremes can create in the child a belief that the world is fundamentally unstable and can change suddenly at any second. This may produce adults who don't try to accomplish their best because they believe it can be suddenly overturned or destroyed—often underlying the inability of a Sun/Uranus person to commit to anything or anyone. The claimed need for "freedom" simply masks the fear that, when one least expects it, the rug will be pulled out. They need to deal directly with the fear of sudden upsets, rather than with the effect. Eclectic therapy can help these people to realize that though the world is unstable, it is not necessarily threatening. Eclectic therapy, utilizing more than one mode or style of therapeutic technique, meets a Uranian need, reflecting an experimental attitude toward life. No one system can fully satisfy Uranians unless they develop it themselves. A philo-sophical awareness that the world has always been undependable, that sudden change is ordinary rather than unusual, will help to calm these fears.

Parents who needlessly restrict Uranian children can expect negative results. Uranian children may benefit from schools with a flexible learning environment where they can function "in their own way" usually at an accelerated pace. Freedom of physical movement is also essential. If forced to sit still and learn in a traditional way, a Uranian child may become an underachiever, as well as a rebel against authority. Sun/Uranus may also be indicative of hyperactivity or of the tendency to respond exaggeratedly to food additives, sugar, or the tensions of modern life.

Sun/Uranus people need to develop some friendships and social connections, rather than only emotionally charged relationships with men who are personally dependable, yet who pursue careers that are unusual or challenging. These contacts can lead to more trust in general and, eventually, to the creation of a base from which to make serious commitments.

MOON/URANUS

The principle of "fluctuation" that affects the physical vehicle with Sun/Uranus contacts in the birth chart also operates with Moon/Uranus, but at an unconscious emotional level. Moon/Uranus people have erratic and volatile patterns of emotional response. Emotions change with rapier-like speed, and these people ride an emotional roller coaster, unaware of how they will react in the next second. Their emotions are easily overstimulated and accelerated; and, they are expressed in totally unexpected directions. Although a situation may remain the same, the Moon/Uranus person will react differently to it from day to day. There are no formulated criteria to govern emotional responses. The enigmatic quality of Uranus negates any attempt to systematize the emotional mechanism. Because their emotional responses are continually diverted by other stimuli, Moon/Uranus people may be accused of a lack of emotional integrity even though their responses are sincere at any given moment. This emotional undependability is not a conscious choice of the Moon/Uranus individual.

Men with Moon/Uranus contacts are usually attracted to emotionally volatile women, those who are very independent and freedom-oriented. Since emotional changeability in women is accepted in our culture, it is easier for Moon/Uranus women to express emotions freely than it is for men. If some Moon/Uranus women perceive themselves as emotionally unstable it's because they are on a perpetual emotional roller coaster. Uranus demands total freedom of expression and compels the Moon to experience every emotion from A to Z and back again at a dizzying speed. Although this can be exciting, it can also leave the woman in a state of disorientation. Because she does not see others in her life reacting so unpredictably, she may consider herself emotionally eccentric or disturbed.

Moon/Uranus individuals need to recognize that cyclic emotional patterns are intrinsic to their nature and perfectly normal for them. Despite their emotional irregularity, these people generally succeed in all their daily activities and are able to maintain healthy relationships with others who accept their up and down emotional patterns. They need to accept their own emotional uniqueness and to stop comparing themselves to others.

When Uranus is in one of its "reversal" stages, it acts like Saturn—withdrawing, becoming rigid. A Moon/Uranus person who has been nurturing and understanding of others suddenly becomes cool and indifferent as the energy reverses itself. Here is the other side of Uranus—an aloofness similar to Saturn. But just wait a bit! Uranus will reverse again, and so will the emotional responses. The emotional dexterity of Moon/Uranus people enables them to be intimate one second, distant the next—which can be tough on relationships. If the Uranian's partner is not sufficiently secure in the relationship (this requires a lot of ego security) he/she can become very disturbed by the mixed messages—these rapidly changing emotional responses. What the partner needs is to develop a healthy indifference. If one focuses too narrowly on one message to the exclusion of the other, then one has lost not only one's perspective of the *total* person but also any ability to deal effectively with the Uranian.

To make Moon/Uranus relationships succeed, the partner needs to be willing to allow the Moon/Uranus person as much emotional freedom or elasticity as needed. Any attempt to confine or limit the Moon/Uranus person emotionally will produce eventual rebellion. If there are Moon and Uranus contacts between their charts, the partners will need to assimilate a good deal of emotional changeability and unpredictability. On the Lunar level, Uranus needs to feel emotionally unencumbered to have the freedom to dynamically experience a wide range of human emotions.

Parents of Moon/Uranus

It is of primary importance for the healthy emotional functioning of Moon/Uranus women to pursue independence and originality in at least one area of their lives. Mothers of today's Moon/Uranus adults rarely had such options. If they appear emotionally unstable or unpredictable today, it may be because they haven't been able to express their own individuality, to make their own stand in the world. Mixed messages from these mothers are, therefore, not un-usual, and they are often very powerful.

Some mothers have chosen to interrupt challenging and suc-cessful careers to raise their children. Or, they have limited their careers rather than let their success exceed that of their husbands' in order to follow cultural role models. As adults, Moon/Uranus men with such mothers will look for women who will make these same sacrifices, and they will become enraged if the women won't. Moon/Uranus women with such mothers find it difficult to commit to family requirements, sensing the emotional cost of such a compromise. Although the strong, self-willed independence of Moon/Uranus women is not acceptable in most segments of our society, it can be an advantage under certain circumstances—in divorce or for the mother who must raise her children without the father's support.

In the same sense that Sun/Uranus children can't depend on consistency in their fathers, Moon/Uranus children will find a lack of consistency in their mothers. Nurturance is erratic, varying from warm and comforting to cool and indifferent. Sometimes the mother is physically absent for periods of time. She may need time to get connected to her own individuality. Or, if she has been work-ing all day, she may find it hard to shift gears quickly enough to meet the child's needs for nurturing. These mothers also experience emo-tional overload faster than other mothers. Shifting gears between family and career can be experienced as an infringement on their basic rights to self-direction and expression. This emotional er-raticism engenders a belief in the child (and, therefore a fear) that nurturance cannot be trusted or depended upon. The result is resistance. To avoid experiencing sudden withdrawal, Moon/Uranus individuals seek their own emotional freedom by accepting the nurturing energy and experiences offered by others, but do not expect its continuance and may withhold nurturance from others, until convinced of their reliability. Ironically, this can create a no-win situation with the Moon/Uranus person waiting and the proposed partner getting the message that no commitment or nurturance is possible. Moon/Uranus people can usually take the chance to show their feelings in such a bind, but they need to do it longer and more often than is their habit. Otherwise the partner doesn't grasp hints, as they flow too quickly for anyone other than another Moon/Uranus to perceive.

MERCURY/URANUS

People with Mercury/Uranus contacts in their birth charts experience being different from others because of their unique mental processes and their way of expressing themselves. As children, their speeded-up thought patterns and modes of communication were dissimilar to others in the family, making them feel uncomfortable. Often they experienced frustration in trying to articulate ideas because their minds moved faster than their mouths. The parents' varying responses to these children were often perplexing. As adults, communication problems may manifest in personal, social and business relationships.

Mercury/Uranus people communicate using a kind of verbal shorthand developed from flashes of insight, a code rarely understood by others. For example, when talking with someone they often jump ahead to make their point, leaving out information essential for understanding. Impatient Uranus short circuits the information process, forgetting that other people have no idea how they arrived at their conclusions. This is why Mercury/Uranus people are so frequently misunderstood, misinterpreted and viewed as ultimately illogical. Their ideas seem to spring out of thin air, they have laid no cohesive groundwork to support their opinions and conclusions.

56 Celestial Psychology

For Uranians to communicate effectively, they must stop assuming others possess mental telepathy. They need to explain or refer to the logical stages in the formulation of their ideas. Reconstructing this mental process for others is a boring and frustrating process for Uranians who have already done this internally. This same mental impatience frequently causes them to interrupt others who are talking. They need to be reminded that others have a right to express themselves in their own way and should be given a fair hearing before the Mercury/Uranus person jumps in. Uranians also have a big stake in shocking and enthralling others with their intellectual acumen and brilliance—something which may be somewhat diminished when exposed to logical thought processes. They may need to choose between spontaneous, brilliant communication that creates misunderstandings, and a less astonishing, but more cogent presentation. Writing can be helpful in establishing effective and logical thought presentations. The process of giving form to ideas requires Mercury/Uranus people to provide all the essential information and to be more attentive to the detailed mental processes.

People with Gemini or Virgo planets or chart angles, or those with Mercury conjunct the Sun, will especially appreciate the "reality" of ideas written down in black and white. Simply keeping a journal can also be helpful in building a more explicit style of communication.

Uranus and Saturn individuals have differing attitudes towards authorities and authoritarianism. In early life, Saturn people believe authorities and are not unduly upset by authoritarian presentations. On the other hand, Uranus individuals rebel against authority figures, especially if they present ideas in an authoritarian manner. As adults, Saturn people become more trusting of their own judgment, once they assume their own positions of authority in life; while Uranians become more trusting of authority figures but never of authoritarians—a distinction they can make easily (except in themselves).

Mercury/Uranus individuals can be very rigid in their thinking. Convinced of their own uniqueness, they tend to reject others' ideas and suggestions, which they believe cannot possibly apply to them. They also assume that if something works well for them, it must be right and will obviously work well for everyone else. After all, they have worked through all possible life situations on a mental level and must have the correct solutions. In a very profound sense, Mercury/Uranus wants to change the world, the current paradigm, the minds of other people. They expect agreement from the people in their lives and become quite disconcerted if they don't receive it. The most effective way to deal with this is to agree with them on a superficial level, unless an important personal principle is involved. It is a way of making them feel accepted and less disassociated from the world. They have permission to be different in an atmosphere that accepts their ideas. Mercury/Uranus people will usually respond with love and warmth. In time, they will even begin to listen to other people's ideas.

Other Mercury/Uranus people have to run every idea through their own internal computer before they can accept its validity. At first, they will reject another person's idea, regardless of its logic or legitimacy. Months later, they may claim the idea as their own, becoming very resentful if their error is pointed out. The end result is the same, but they have to go through their own judgment and evaluation process.

Mercury/Uranus people are inquisitive and experimental. They like to explore many varied intellectual areas, especially if it is their idea. Someone else's idea should be presented in a "what if . . ." manner, which stimulates their curiosity. When they are older, they may be more accepting of outside ideas, but only from recognized and respected authorities on a subject, who appeal to Mercury/Uranus because they have experienced, not just presented theory.

Mercury/Uranus is also very objective in solving emotional problems for others because of their unique perspective. Uranians can come up with solutions that are quite inventive and helpful. However, when they try to apply this to their own emotional situations, the problem-solving mechanism breaks down. In emotional situations they respond as subjectively as anyone around them.

VENUS/URANUS

Love at first sight, a bolt from the blue! That's a Venus/Uranus contact! Believe it or not, all that instant attraction is powered from the mental plane. Venus can be very intellectual through its rulership of Libra and very sensual through its rulership of Taurus. The sexual attraction of Venus/Uranus contacts starts with a "mental" trigger. Venus/Uranus people are often stimulated by another's brilliance, by someone, for instance, who has done exceptional work in their own field. (I know so many women who attend lectures and go absolutely *ga ga* over the male speaker who says something they've never heard before!) The problem begins, however, when they try to transfer all that mental intimacy to the physical level. Venus/Uranus people, whether sexually stimulated or not, have a romantic impulse toward the person giving them information. But these relationships are often short-lived because Uranus is satiated quickly. The passion subsides, although it can be overwhelmingly exciting while it's happening.

Venus/Uranus individuals may have problems related to physical intimacy and closeness. Sometimes they don't want to be touched, except in sexual situations. Or, they can be physically expressive one moment, aloof the next. They are extremely intense when attracted to a person, either intellectually or romantically (love at first sight), but this intensity usually burns out within a few months, sometimes sooner. This illustrates the Uranian reversal, the sudden on-off syndrome and the need to be free. It is helpful to remember that Uranus' rulership of Aquarius signifies friendship. Venus/Uranus people need to recognize that they may get what they are looking for in friendship rather than in emotional commitment or romance. Yet, it may be hard for them to distinguish between the two. Unless they can define objective parameters for their relationship, both partners will experience much pain and dissatisfaction because of contradictory expectations.

People with Venus/Uranus contacts often form cross-cultural relationships. This is also true with Venus contacts to the other outer planets, the 5th and 7th houses, but the reasons are different. The Uranus attraction may have its base in teen-age rebellion. How strong the attraction is probably depends on how much the parents object to the relationship and try to squash it (or would if they knew of it). If Venus/Uranus people feel their individuality is being strongly restricted by their parents, they may consciously choose someone they know their parents are going to hate. If their parents have a "button" about Arabians, for sure they will find an Arabian to fall in love with.

Parental approbation aside, Venus/Uranus individuals may select someone who is unacceptable *to themselves*. If they don't feel secure about their own background, they will never choose someone from the same background. "If I'm not okay, then you can't be okay, either," they reason. However, these relationships rarely last long. The partners may be unwilling to resolve what they regard as "irreconcilable" differences in attitude. There is no conflict during the initial stages of attraction, but when they marry or live together, they encounter each other directly and must reach some sort of compromise or cooperation. The success of such a relationship is contingent upon each person's commitment to accommodate differences and to permit social freedom for each other. Such freedom cannot be scheduled as that is too Saturnian. It must be a condition of the relationship that each person is free to pursue his/her own interests—even unexpectedly.

Hopefully, as Venus/Uranus individuals grow older, they work through their rebellious instincts and come to discover they can be compatible with others from their own background. No longer prodded by rebellion, their desire for "different" people often wanes. As they become more accepting of their own background, they can, eventually, establish relationships with those of the same or similar background.

Venus/Uranus people need to change their attitudes toward relationships. Even if there is resistance, Uranus will keep hammering away until changes are made. The lesson to be learned is *universal* love, not *personal* love. Uranus, like Neptune and Pluto, is an impersonal planet. Its contact with a personal planet implies learning a personal lesson concerning society at large. Universal love, in the nonpersonal sense, is represented by Venus/Uranus. When Venus contacts Uranus, the sexuality of Venus is expanded to include a broader, less specific expression of love.

Conception and Childbirth

Venus/Uranus contacts are often present in charts of pregnancies usually connected to the Moon by transit, progression or solar arc. (Miscarriage can also occur under Venus/Uranus due to possible erratic functioning.) One of the literal meanings of Venus/Uranus is conception. When a woman discovers she is pregnant, her reaction is often one of surprise (Uranus), even though she may also be very pleased. Venus is also associated with creativity, so the conception doesn't need to be physical (especially with the birth control methods available today). Venus/Uranus conception energy can be channeled into creative areas (designated by Venus' house position and rulership, natally and by progression) where it can mark the start of highly significant endeavors.

MARS/URANUS

Mars/Uranus energy is comparable to that of a high tension wire, which makes it very difficult to control. This explosive combination of planets has a reputation for producing hair-trigger tempers and sudden, explosive anger. In our society, it is not always acceptable to express anger openly or with any regularity. This may explain some of the international conflict in our world. Wars are a manifestation of collective anger, anger projected from a mass of people. But this is difficult to see because Uranus detaches from acknowledging personal anger, and from dealing with it on an individual level.

Impulsive or rash action is also common with Mars/Uranus contacts. When angry, these people frequently say things they are sorry for later. Then, if pride gets in the way of an apology or explanation, relationships may be broken off. If, however, they can use the reversal mechanism of Uranus to pre-program themselves, they'll be able to halt in mid-tirade and let the other person know at once that they don't mean it.

Anger creates such extreme muscular tension in Mars/Uranus people that it can literally cause the body to shake. If this anger is not diffused or mitigated to some extent, then it may be uncontrollably unleashed, often in the form of an accident. Typically, Mars/Uranus people are accident-prone. They collect burns, bruises and cuts. Motorized vehicles are particularly hazardous for them if they haven't taken steps to release their pent-up anger effectively. They may drive with complete safety until they get angry. Then, if they won't talk about it or take some steps to work off the anger, they may have an accident. I had a client who was a traveling salesman. Every two years, like clockwork, he had an accident as transiting

Mars triggered his Mars/Uranus. People with Mars/Uranus natally or by transit need to go out and run around the block, pound the walls, yell and scream, do whatever is necessary to release anger before they drive.

The seriousness of the internal tension and corresponding anger can be measured by the damage done to the body. Men especially tend to identify their bodies with their cars. The motor vehicle becomes a mechanical extension of their own physical vehicle. This is why it is so important to drain off any residual internal tension before driving. Mars/Uranus people may also encounter mechanical problems with their vehicles—cars break down instead of having accidents. Symbolically, these people feel their own drive and initiative is not dependable and will break down. If they continually encounter accidents or mechanical breakdowns in life, there is some internal complex that is not being given adequate attention. External circumstances simply show them how they are misdirecting or misusing personal energy. An accident is the symbolic example of a personal situation that is out of control. Once the individual confronts and resolves the internal problem, the energy ceases to cause havoc on the material plane.

When Mars/Uranus people also have a prominent Pluto or Saturn, the problem is one of *overcontrolling* anger. Saturn puts on the brakes and Pluto may bury; so, the anger is directed inward, creating potential health problems. The circumstances generating anger must be rectified. If the problem is an unhealthy relationship or job situation, breaking the ties may be the only way to break the tension. Mars/Uranus individuals who appear calm and relaxed are those who have taken steps to resolve their anger in a positive manner.

Therapeutic Techniques

A therapist I know advocates an interesting exercise to handle Mars/Uranus energy when it becomes extremely intense. She suggests that clients should wait until they are alone at home. They lie down, kick their legs, bang their fists, and generally try to provoke a temper tantrum. Initially, they may feel a little foolish, but in a few minutes, they get into the swing of it — yelling, screaming, crying, allowing themselves to become as violent as needed. They are letting their anger out, giving themselves the Uranian freedom to express it openly and safely. Anger is thus liberated, and not channeled into accidents or in other directions that may be self-destructive or hurtful to another person. This exercise is an excellent way for these people to acknowledge anger consciously, rather than let it run away with them.

The physical activities discussed with regard to Sun/Uranus are equally appropriate for Mars/Uranus contacts. Uranus physically stimulates the musculature; so, all forms of rigorous exercise, particularly competitive (Mars) activity, would be advantageous. Mars/Uranus people have to drain off energy on a daily basis, before it becomes stored up and is manifested in the more deleterious ways. Physical activity need not be overly structured or disciplined. Any activity involved with exerting force and movement would be helpful. Cleaning house, washing the car, running around the room, jumping up and down or beating a pillow are all forms of tension release available to people at any time. Several Mars/Uranus men I know have taken up boxing to redirect their anger.

Uranus predisposes Martian energy to be spasmodic; correspondingly, sexual energy is sporadic. Truly creative people, whether they make a living by their creative processes or not, often are not interested in sexual expression while they are creating. The physical sexual energy of Mars is transmuted into creative energy. Although this can occur with Mars/Neptune, it is the Mars/Uranus either-or/on-off circuitry that temporarily diverts the sexual energy.

Men with Mars/Uranus contacts will opt for creative over sexual activity or vice versa. Women with Mars/Uranus are often quite perturbed when their male partners apparently become disinterested in sexual activity during creative periods. Conversely, Mars/Uranus women may detach themselves from sexual expression (for obvious physiological reasons, women can be receptive even when not mentally inclined, while men cannot). Regardless of who expresses the Mars/Uranus energy, both partners must understand the on-again/off-again pattern of sexual activity and learn to deal with its implications.

Mars/Uranus people are often attracted to different forms of sexual expression than those they knew about when they were growing up. This should not be construed as an interest in unorthodox sexual activity, *per se*. The primary focus is on experiencing many different types of sexual activity. As with Venus/Uranus contacts, the difference is relative to the individual's background. The nonverbal messages the young child receives in the early home environment engender a specific perspective on sexuality. A person raised on a farm in the Midwest is going to have a different sexual perspective than someone raised in an urban environment. The farm individual has a more realistic biological grasp of sexuality, while the urban person's understanding of sexuality is more laced with social factors. One can only infer that Mars/Uranus individuals (or those with Uranus in the 8th or 5th houses) are going to be attracted to something different from what they were exposed to in the past.

Often they are attracted to opposite values from their parents, which may be a symbol of rebellion. Children born during the 1940's and 1950's rebelled *en masse* against the standards of their parents born during the 1920's and 1930's. Today's young adults tend to be fairly conservative, a Uranian rebellion against the parents responsible for overturning some of society's most conventional establishment rules. Feeling there is nothing to rebel against, some have become ultraconservative. Uranus is going to rebel, no matter what; thus, a liberal parent will wind up with a conservative child!

JUPITER/URANUS

Jupiter/Uranus is the proverbial lucky combination. Jupiter represents luck, and the Jupiter/Uranus contact increases that luck exponentially. People who have interactions between the Sun and Jupiter/Uranus have been known to total a car and walk away without a scratch. Having a Jupiter/Uranus contact is like being "saved in the nick of time." Men stationed at the front lines during wartime, who came through it safely despite being inundated with bombs, most assuredly have Jupiter/Uranus contacting their Sun, Midheaven, Sun/Midheaven midpoint, or possibly their Ascendant. An aspect of Jupiter to Uranus protects a person from the more perilous and life-threatening circumstances, although the Uranian may be accident-prone in a minor sense. The greater the danger, the more this Jupiter/Uranus contact is going to be of assistance. It is fascinating to examine these contacts in the charts of heavily Saturnian people. Because of the Saturn "worry mechanism", they tend not to recognize the assistance from unexpected sources that they receive through Jupiter/Uranus contacts.

Individuals with Jupiter contacting Uranus are somewhat predisposed to handle money in an erratic manner. Jupiter symbolizes money, and the nature of Uranus inclines the person toward impulse buying and spending. That on/off Uranian switch implies that they can be very careful with money at times. Then, when the switch is activated, they will spend money quickly and lavishly. Gambling may be an important part of their lifestyle.

Jupiter/Uranus individuals are often led to explore new philosophical or metaphysical systems. They enjoy expanding their consciousness and awareness in life, and they usually become involved in spreading the light they receive to others. They may become torchbearers in their immediate circle or involve themselves in social reform. Typical of Uranus however, no one belief system or philosophy will be fully satisfying. Uranian individuals need to be eclectic, combining the information and techniques from more than one system to develop a workable philosophy for themselves.

URANUS/NEPTUNE

Because Uranus, Neptune and Pluto are all planets of cosmic consciousness, contacts between them are extremely important. Since they are slow-moving, millions of people are born with these planets in aspect to each other. Those with Uranus/Neptune contacts aspecting personal points or planets will tend to "personalize" the energy and develop a metaphysical attitude toward life. Without these aspects, individuals tend to associate with others who have a peripheral interest in metaphysics or the paranormal. Hard aspects make the influence more prominent and more likely to manifest externally. The softer contacts are aspects of inclination and are less likely to materialize externally.

Uranus/Neptune contacts represent altered states of consciousness, which can be induced in many ways. Being unconscious is an altered state, whether it is caused by overindulgence in drugs or alcohol (anesthetized) or by being knocked unconscious. Most importantly, when Uranus/Neptune contacts aspect any personal points or planets, these people should exercise extreme caution concerning their intake of synthetic substances. Uranus indicates a reaction to drugs that is contrary to medical expectations, while Neptune suggests the possibility that illness or disease may be mis-diagnosed (they should always obtain a second opinion). These people are extremely sensitive and susceptible to drugs, whether used therapeutically or for recreation. The drug/alcohol experience for Uranus/Neptune people can be quite unpleasant. While uncon-scious, they are open to attracting negative energy which can pro-duce bizarre behavior or *extra-ordinary* mental perspectives.

Sleep and meditation are more positive altered states of con-sciousness. Uranus/Neptune contacts to personal planets or points can produce trance mediums of various types. Some fall into very deep trances, while others go into relatively light states of trance. The light trance person usually has a strong Saturn or Pluto which prevents the loss of control inherent in the deeper trance states.

Experiencing these altered states is almost unavoidable for those wtih Uranus/Neptune contacts to their personal planets or points. Others not exposed to the metaphysical world may view them as psychotic. As a counselor, I have seen cases where people with these contacts experience communications, images and actual contacts with deceased parents or loved ones who have died re-cently. These experiences may so disturb their overall functioning that they are institutionalized temporarily or sedated because they are unable to cope. If Pluto is involved in this complex, then contact with the "unseen" world of gods, goddesses, demons, ghosts or other super-natural beings is indicated.

Uranus/Neptune contacts can also mark conflict between the desire to be free within a social context (Uranus) and the feeling of obligation to society (Neptune). According to Sabian astrology, these planets form planetary pairs (similar to Jupiter/Saturn and Venus/Mars) and planetary pairs always produce conflict and con-trast. Both Uranus and Neptune correlate with astrology. There are numerous Uranus/Neptune connections to points/Planets in the charts of professional astrologers. Astrologically, there is conflict between humanistic astrology (Neptune) and technological astrology (Uranus). The humanists may disregard the importance of new procedures and calculations, while the technocrats may miss the validity of the psychological approach. Naturally, the two must interface to gain the greatest benefit for astrology.

Uranus/Neptune contacts and midpoints are often found in the charts of disasters in which a number of people are killed. People who die in airplane crashes, bomb raids or any catastrophic event usually have a Uranus/Neptune aspect or midpoint in contact with their Sun or Ascendant at the time of the disaster.

URANUS/PLUTO

Uranian change is always subject to reversal. But the change implied by Pluto is far more dynamic and inclusive, altering one's life irrevocably. Uranus may change a situation, inject new information, but Pluto can eliminate the situation altogether.

People with Uranus/Pluto contacts may not have fit into their family or may never have conformed to their early environment. This is especially true if the planets contact personal points or planets. Throughout their lives, these people attempt to change the world around them in an effort to feel more comfortable and at ease in it. These changes are usually accomplished with upheaval—an earthquake, if you like. They move, change partners, mates, jobs, careers, friends, all at once. These sudden shifts may occur with some frequency in the first half of life, then become less frequent as they grow older (having experimented sufficiently to be sure of their preferences in life-style, career, etc.). When both these planets contact personal planets and points, the individual is a trail blazer and role-model in life. Often, such people will continue to make unusual life adjustments into their 60's, 70's or beyond.

People with Uranus/Pluto contacts that don't aspect personal planets or points may be interested in changing the world, but they rarely feel compelled to institute the change themselves.

On a mundane level, when Uranus entered Libra, people began to live together rather than being sanctioned in marriage. They rebelled against conventional Libran partnerships and marriage in an attempt to achieve social freedom. Then, when Uranus entered Scorpio, many of these people decided to get married.

Pluto's transit through Libra has accomplished a good deal of reform in the laws governing marriage and divorce, including the "no-fault" divorce. Also, there is now a greater awareness of the different forms of marriage that are possible. People are able to form premarital agreements concerning each person's money and property. These are all examples of Uranus' and Pluto's influence in changing our perspective on relationships and marriage. When the children who were born with these placements become adults, we can expect to see even greater reform in these areas.

CHAPTER 4

NEPTUNE

Neptune symbolizes our ideals, dreams, aspirations and our concepts of purity and perfection. It envisions an alternate reality or state of eternal spiritual bliss. The Neptunian reality is not composed of matter and form, it is transphysical and cannot be experienced on the material plane. People encounter resistance when they attempt to experience this alternate reality on the material plane. Perfection and purity are incapable of survival in the world of dense matter, although people constantly strive toward these ideals on the physical level. It is as though we remember experiencing another level of consciousness and Neptune entices us to try to attain it while in the body. Neptune promises us another world, a more perfect and beautiful reality where our needs are automatically fulfilled and we are all united in the state of Nirvana. There are probably only two occasions when a human being may have experienced a similar state of Nirvana. During gestation our needs are fulfilled without even asking and at the end of life we may be on medical life-support systems that provide the same type of maintenance for the physical vehicle. At both these times, we are not responsible for our physical survival which allows us to enter into the Neptunian realm.

The process of meditation can alter our consciousness and bring us closer to the Neptunian reality. It opens us up to a world not ruled by physical matter, but by spiritual ideals and concepts. Individuals with a prominent Neptune have the capacity to be spiritual and to be committed to a higher ideal. This is the most positive expression of Neptunian energy. It is extremely inspirational, imaginative, creative and spiritual. If we involve ourselves in activities of that nature, the energy gradually filters down onto the material plane. The energy needs to be focused in these areas to manifest positively to avoid the rather difficult facets intrinsic to Neptune.

Neptune's influence convinces people that the alternate state of reality is more real than this plane of existence. Yet, there is nothing to represent it in tangible form. Neptune is not particularly happy or comfortable being earthed and limited to the physical world. Sometimes, people with strong Neptune influences in their charts may attempt to ground the energy and make it objectively real. On the material plane, Neptune represents chemicals or pollutants, and people often are seduced into using Neptunian substances such as alcohol and drugs to their disadvantage. These products are impure, sometimes chemically synthesized. They create a state of disillusion and separation from reality—a distorted replication of the Neptunian reality. It is an unfortunate and deluded attempt to escape this reality with the hope of reaching the promised land of Neptune.

Neptune is related to the concept of deception or misrepresentation. A person may sometimes deliberately plan to deceive other people, but frequently the Neptunian has deceived him/herself, and other people are exposed to it in this manner. It is perhaps true that only a person who possesses the ability to deceive can be deceived by another. All of us have the ability to deceive whether or not we decide to use it. If a person has been seriously deceived in some situation, it is important to realize that it was not because he or she is inherently evil and planned to deceive someone else. A person is often deceived because of his or her naiveté, and it should not be construed as a form of punishment.

Neptune dissolves the identification of the self with the ego. People tend to identify and define themselves with their bodies, emotions and thoughts, and these are components of the ego as it relates to Saturnian reality. The self is correlated with a person's spirit, essence or soul. Thoughts, emotions and physicality are *manifestations* of the self—they belong to the self but do not define it. People can become overly attached to their emotions and allow those emotions to define them. Neptune compels us to realize that our real "selves" are simply experiencing the difficult mental emotional and physical levels of material existence and in order to give up or relinquish our identification with them.

The birthchart elucidates how a person is plugged into experience on those levels because it symbolizes a kind of celestial machinery. Transits, progressions and solar arc directions illustrate how the machinery is functioning at a specific point of existence; although, it is impossible to discover at what point a person is in his/her spiritual development. It is impossible to predict how a person will navigate a period of transition because the self/spirit is not identifiable in the birthchart. Neptune represents spirituality, but not a measurable spiritual quotient. The charts of astro-twins can produce very similar events but their reactions to the same life circumstances will be different—the two people have different souls at different stages of spiritual development.

The mirror effect of Neptune functions as both a reflection of ourselves in the world, (as when we look into a mirror), and also as a projection of ourselves (as when light reflects off a mirror).

Because Neptune is noted for its "cloudiness," we think we see others when we look into the mirror when actually we see ourselves. This means that the behavior or circumstances that distress us are actually that which we refuse to acknowledge as our own or to clean up; and so, it returns to us from others. This is most often seen clearly in situations with people with whom we are not close. For instance, you get up feeling angry and continually encounter anger in others during the day. For those people with whom we have strong connections, Neptune often functions by our taking on both their positive and negative qualities. When we take on a positive quality of another, we reflect it back into the world. This can be seen when the Neptunian person begins to speak or behave in the same manner as those with whom they associate. When we take on the negative qualities of others we experience pain, distress, discomfort and sometimes agony, as we process that quality forcing a definition of self.

SUN/NEPTUNE

Sun/Neptune contacts indicate a high degree of physical sensitivity, causing the body to suffer periodic declines. The Sun represents our physical vitality; Mars, our energy level. With Sun/Neptune it is possible to have high Martian energy, while the basic life force is depleted. Under Mars/Neptune this is reversed; the energy level can be somewhat diminished, while the physical vitality may be unaffected.

Because of their physical sensitivity, Sun/Neptune individuals should use caution in ingesting all Neptunian substances, from drugs and alcohol to preservatives and coloring agents used in food preparation. Because Neptune is associated with chemicals and synthetic substances, all Sun/Neptune people are inclined to overreact physically to foods with a high chemical content. They are predisposed to allergic reactions. The Sun/Neptune contact defines the primary allergic or addictive personality. Allergies can include environmental pollutants, such as insecticides so commonly used on fruits and vegetables. Sun/Neptune people are advised to wash food carefully before eating, to remove any residual surface chemicals; and to read food labels, thus cutting down the intake of additives and preservatives. The inscrutable quality of Neptune makes it even more difficult to identify the pernicious effects of various chemicals. Other common pollutants and toxins to be avoided as much as possible include: air pollution, simple house dust, insect sprays, weed killers and household cleaning agents.

Sun/Neptune people may also have an unpredictable reaction to drugs and alcohol, predicated on their sensitivity at the time of ingestion. At one time, they may be intoxicated after only one drink; while at another time, they can have many drinks without the same effect. In either case, they may suffer few hangover symptoms, although their vitality will be depleted for days while processing the Neptunian substance. Tobacco is another drug that can wear down physical vitality. The first cigarette usually causes dizziness and coughing. If Sun/Neptune individuals monitored their physical reactions, and paid attention to their bodies messages, they would be able to establish workable limits for the use of drugs, alcohol, tobacco, etc. A good rule for Sun/Neptune people is that if nothing happens with one or two drinks or puffs of marijuana, they should stop before they drain their vitality. If, on the other hand, they get "high" quickly, it's not necessary to continue. They are already experiencing the desired effect.

Individuals with Sun/Neptune contacts, or Neptune in or ruling the 1st or 6th house or connected to planets in the 1st or 6th houses, should also give special attention to the quality of their professional health care and treatment. Because Neptune tends to mask the true cause, doctors may misdiagnose physical ailments and diseases. To ensure proper diagnoses and treatment, Sun/Neptune people should obtain a second opinion. If the second opinion contradicts the initial diagnosis, then they should get a third opinion. Because it may take a long time to discover the root cause of an illness or disease, Sun/Neptune people should seek the highest level of medical care that does not unthinkingly adhere to textbook learning. They should not be misled by medical omnipotence or by doctors who are too eager to assess a problem without adequate investigation.

On another level, Sun/Neptune represents the astral body. Because Neptunian products affect the astral body before they arrive on the physical plane, homeopathy may be the most successful form of treatment. It is assumed that homeopathic preparations treat the astral body first, then filter down to the physical vehicle. They trigger the Neptune mechanism to correct physical imbalance. Their subtle action is sympathetic to the nature of Neptune and doesn't devastate the sensitive Neptunian body. Allopathic drugs (those most commonly used in the medical community) are always antithetical to the nature of the disease. They confront it directly, which may be too forceful for the Neptunian. Homeopathic drugs are far more refined, contain traces similar to the agents found in the disease, and work from the assumption that "like cures like." Their action is similar to that of vaccines, but is much more subtle and less concentrated.

Sun/Neptune Fathers

Sun/Neptune people (male and female) often become involved with men who aren't dependable, and this starts with Dad. Although the father may not be physically absent, he may be inattentive or unaware of the child's needs, especially problems with other family members. Sun/Neptune people often have alcoholic fathers or, in a more contemporary vein, fathers with marijuana or drug problems. In any case, the father's attention is somehow diverted from the child's needs; the child feels a lack of support from the father, and perceives him as indifferent to his/her needs. This indifference affects the child's sense of direction. It is as if anything the child does, or hopes to become, is acceptable to the father; the child is neither encouraged or discouraged. Often this leads to such children feeling invisible and powerless so that in adult life there is often a tendency to escape facing this theme within themselves by seeking to save others. These children are in a kind of psychic limbo, never sure of who they are, where to focus their identity, or how to receive support.

Since Neptune represents the ideal, its connection to Sun, Moon, the 4th and 10th houses can produce a condition in which the individual doesn't see the parent clearly, even in later life. The parent (usually of the opposite sex) is thought to be all that is good, kind, even saintly.

This is as deleterious a situation as its reverse and requires a concentrated effort to see the true humanity of the parent, rather than the original immature image. Without this accurate perception, the Neptune person goes through life being bitterly disappointed that men or women aren't as "good" as the parent. This projection of the potential image onto another person is typical of the "pretty picture" need of Neptune.

Neptunian people frequently want to save the world, a noble and altruistic ideal, but one that frequently creates problems in relationships. Women with Sun/Neptune or Mars/Neptune often become romantically involved with charming, but undependable men, or those who have addictive tendencies. Neptune is the "savior"— so they try to save the man. Conversely, these women seek men who will save *them*. (The same instincts are present in men with Moon/Neptune or Venus/Neptune, who seek women to save or to be saved by.) Always, the woman is projecting her unconscious image of man's potential onto the man with whom she is involved.

Sun/Neptune people who try to help or save others risk involving themselves in a *savior/martyr/victim* complex. Neptunians are able to empathize with other's problems in a very profound way, to identify with pain to such an extent that they embody it. This process is automatic and relatively unconscious. Therefore, people with Sun/Neptune (or Neptune contacts to personal planets or points) are privy to everyone's problems. People constantly unload on them a litany of painful experiences. And, because of boundless sympathy, the Neptunian is willing to listen.

In the *savior* phase of the complex, Sun/Neptune people identify with the problem, feeling all the concomitant emotions; then, they offer advice and seek to save the person. When that person ignores their advice, or talks endlessly about the problem without attempting to resolve it, they feel taken advantage of and martyred. They are disappointed because the other person didn't live up to their idealistic image.

When they continue to offer advice that is ignored, they enter the *victim* stage of the complex. Anyone attempting to save another risks becoming addicted to that person and to his/her problem. They are victimized because their expectations and solutions are not the same as those of the person they are trying to rescue. Neptunian people need to stop identifying so closely with problems they don't own. There is a difference between help and assistance, sympathy and compassion. People addicted to their own sympathetic instincts cannot be objective. Whereas those acting from compassion can acknowledge another's problem, be of assistance, and still maintain a healthy distance. Compassion recognizes a problem but doesn't become absorbed by it. Because of their extreme susceptibility and receptiveness, Sun/Neptune people need to put a healthy distance between themselves and others in order to maintain their individuality, and avoid being submerged in the other person's life, even if there is no negative condition present.

Victimization either by individuals or by conditions can manifest as physical fatigue. Victimized Sun/Neptune or Mars/Neptune people or those with Neptune angular sacrifice their vitality to others, and this can happen as easily by telephone as in person. Sun/Neptune people may wake up feeling well rested and lively, then be drained by the time they reach their office. Like a sponge, they have absorbed all the vibrations in the environment, whether the energy was directed at them or not. There is no conscious control in this process; people exchange energy constantly through a circuit functioning on an unconscious level. The most obvious energy exchanges occur between parent and child, close friends, mates or anyone with whom a person has frequent contact.

When there is a close connection between Neptune people and those who are ill, the Neptunian may be drained of energy during sleep. They go to sleep feeling fine, while the ill person suffers from depleted vitality. In the morning, the situation is often reversed. The Neptunian feels more tired than before going to bed, the ill person feels recharged. A one-sided flow of energy from the Neptune person to the ill person has occurred during the sleep state. Sometimes an ill person deliberately takes energy (psychic vampirism), but more often the desire is unconscious. What is important is the deep, unconscious interconnection. Whether the Neptunian's energy is sought unconsciously or is given freely, it flows one way—from the Neptunian to the other person.

People in "helping" professions are subject to these vitality drains because of the nature of their work. They involve themselves with the mental, emotional and physical problems of others and may allow their own vitality to be transferred during the healing process. This is not to imply that Neptunians shouldn't give energy to others; but, they should be careful not to exhaust their own supply. There is an abundance of energy in the universe from innumerable sources. Neptune people should not feel guilty about conserving their own since they need it for personal survival.

Therapeutic Techniques

An excellent visualization technique, designed to protect the aura (electromagnetic field surrounding the body) from unwanted outside influences, is known as the *auric egg*. Neptunian people should imagine they are surrounded by an egg composed of gold filagree. As they visualize this egg covering their heads and extending under their feet, they should suggest to themselves that "Only good gets in and only good gets out." If they have experienced energy drains, they should reaffirm that their energy is to stay with them. The egg should then be flooded with a golden white light. Gold is suggested because it is kinder to the sensitive vehicle of the Neptune person than is a brilliant white light. In cases of physical depletion, the egg should be filled with a clear, green light, since this is the all-purpose healing color. The egg is transportable, it moves anywhere a person chooses to go, and it works for approximately 12 hours. The auric egg is particularly useful for Neptunian types living with an ill person. The egg makes it possible for them to send healing energy to others without sacrificing their own. They can mentally send golden light to the ill person, imagining it surrounding that person. The important distinction here is that they are sending energy they have directed from the cosmos, and not energy drained from themselves. An *auric egg* can also be visualized before going to sleep. It may be as large as the person desires, even surrounding the entire house.

Creativity, associated with Neptune, may be used to restore vitality. Music, for instance, revitalizes and recharges people, consequently restoring their balance. People may become revitalized by listening to their favorite music, visiting museums, galleries or by looking at art books (all Neptunian activities). Any creative activity, such as, singing, dancing, drawing, painting, redecorating the home, will also be beneficial. Movies are related to Neptune; therefore, watching an inspiring movie may be yet another way to recharge energy.

Counseling astrologers may absorb vibrations from clients when they are dealing with serious problem situations. If sympathy has overcome compassion, astrologers can pick up residual feelings from the client, feelings that promote worry—especially if the counselors have an active Saturn or Pluto. They may become overly concerned about situations in their own lives that have previously not bothered them at all. Perhaps the best (and certainly the most available) remedy to detach from borrowed emotions is to take a shower. Be sure to wash your hair. Negative vibrations can become trapped here. Water is related to emotion, and Neptune, ruler of a water sign, refers to cleansing and purification. People who prefer to bathe should take a shower following their bath; otherwise, they just sit in water filled with the negative vibrations that they are trying to get rid of. If it is not possible to shower, they should wash their hands. This removes some of the "sticky" vibrations from the body. While water flows over their hands or body, they should renounce the attachment to another's vibrations and visualize these being washed off. People employed in the helping/healing professions should wash their hands between each client's session to eradicate any residual emotional attachments. Strongly Neptunian people, or those with an emphasis in Virgo (sign opposite Pisces, ruled by Neptune) do take frequent showers. Others may think that they are obsessed with cleanliness or that they have a psychological dislike of dirt. Some do, but showers or washing often make them feel better, emotionally and mentally.

MOON/NEPTUNE

Similar to the Sun/Neptune correspondence to an addictive father/ male family figure, Moon/Neptune contacts often indicate an alco- holic or addictive mother/female family figure. The mother's addic- tive activities may range from overindulgence in alcohol or drugs, to "missions" or general inattentiveness. If unemployed, the mother may drink in the presence of the child or she may try to hide her drinking. The mother may also be a television or telephone addict, or use religious/spiritual affiliations to escape. In each case, her attention is diverted from the child. If Neptune is retrograde, the mother may be extremely religious, very self-righteous, and possibly see herself as a martyr.

Women with Moon/Neptune contacts may be addictive them- selves or involved with other women who are. Men with Moon/ Neptune may encounter these problems with their mothers or other women in their lives. The positive side of Moon/Neptune contacts can be seen in those who are highly creative, artistic, or who possess strong spiritual inclinations that are neither rigid, dogmatic nor asso- ciated with martyrdom.

Because the Moon is involved with heightened perception, people with Moon/Neptune contacts (or Moon in Pisces) may be very psychic. They are able to perceive very subtle and intangible energies in their environment, especially those with emotional over- tones. Psychic perception is not synonymous with intuition. They have different receptive qualities. Intuition is related to Uranus be- cause it is sharp, clear and direct. It comes like a bolt of lightning, intense, quick and brilliant. Psychic perception, on the other hand, is more ambiguous. It lacks the clarity and precision of intuition. Moon/Neptune people receive impressions and feelings that are difficult to define or identify. They are always accompanied by fuzziness, uncertainty or confusion. Neptunians operate on another level of consciousness, psychically tuned to higher, more subtle vibrations.

Because their emotional mechanisms are so finely tuned and sensitized to others, Moon/Neptune people are very effective in the helping professions. The same Neptunian energy that may disorient or confuse them, can be redirected for the purpose of helping others. From the birth chart, one cannot tell which direction the energy will take—patient or therapist. Many therapists have previously undergone therapy. But people with a strong Neptune want to assist (sometimes save) others in distress on all levels—spiritual, mental, emotional and physical. Those interested in helping on the socio-economic level become social workers. We usually think of social workers as having a strong Uranus. This may be true, but Uranians are more often motivated to change the system. Social workers seek to change the person. Neptune is a social planet in the largest sense. It is interested in saving the world and people, not necessarily in changing them.

Moon/Neptune people tend to be emotionally romantic about their ideals, which leads to some unrealistic expectations. Since Neptune consistently promises more than the world can deliver, they need to develop some perspective about their aspirations. Moon/Neptune people are particularly disheartened when they attempt to focus their dreamy ideals in personal situations. To work toward manifesting a social ideal is high-minded, but to attempt to manifest a personal ideal can be unfortunate and disappointing. Outer planet energies are best expressed within the impersonal social context. It is virtually impossible to establish a personal relationship or any situation that will fulfill the idealistic expectations of Neptune. Perfection and idealism are Neptunian concepts not available on the material plane at this stage of human evolution. As long as Neptunian people strive toward unrealistic goals, they will be repeatedly disappointed and disillusioned. Ultimately, they arrive at awareness, but it can be a very painful and disheartening process.

Moon/Neptune women are so sensitive to the emotional states of others, especially their lovers or mates, that they take on and reflect the wishes and desires of those people important in their lives. Although this can make for a highly-charged romantic affair, ultimately the danger of the woman not knowing whether she is acting or being her own real self looms large. This total submergence doesn't usually last and the end of it can be disappointment for the other person involved as he or she had been led to believe that the Moon/Neptune person really was totally in tune with them. As always with Neptune, the individuals owning the contact need to define for themselves who they are and be sure to let others experience them as clearly as possible.

Those Moon/Neptune people who have been extremely hurt, who have seen life-long dreams shattered, or come to realize their dreams might never be fulfilled, tend to hold onto their disappointments and hide them from the world. The Moon retains emotion, and Neptune masks and camouflages true feeling. These people tend to withdraw from life, to stay home as much as possible, to refuse phone calls or any connection with the outside world. (This can be a phase in the healing process.) Withdrawal periods are frequently timed by a Neptune transit. From the time it moves within a two-degree orb of aspect, it takes about one-and-a-half years to complete the contact. The "one-and-a-half" period seems to apply differently, depending on the seriousness of the emotional wound. People will withdraw for one-and-a-half days or one-and-a-half weeks, if the unpleasant situation is relatively minor. If the emotional pain is greater, they may withdraw for one-and-a-half months. When withdrawal continues for one-and-a-half years, the problem is serious. Withdrawal has become a lifestyle and refuge from the world. They may be using such Neptunian escape mechanisms as sleeping through the day or sedating themselves with television. If they do get involved in some external Neptune activity such as a concert or movie, they will often withdraw again when they return home. These people are afraid to confront the outside world, they fear being hurt again. If they are unwilling to come out from withdrawal after one-and-a-half years, they will need assistance to become involved again in the experience of living. Moon/Neptune people desperately need the support and encouragement of close friends and family, to re-establish connections with others and to regain their sense of confidence. If family and friends are not available to help, they should seek professional therapeutic assistance.

Apathy is a Neptunian response to the harshness of unkindness of the real world, contrary to the hope for the ideal. Many Moon/

Neptune or other sensitive Neptune types retreat into apathy and indifference to anesthetize themselves to life. Even fanatic adherence to a cult may be a preferable Neptune response to being wounded; but, most Neptune people will need some period of retreat and withdrawal to heal. Care should be taken not to "get stuck" there.

Moon/Neptune people need detachment through tuning into a larger view, not withdrawal. Detachment makes it possible to function in the world and still live a highly creative and productive life. Detachment is a positive expression of the Neptunian need to protect oneself from absorbing negative energy. Long-term withdrawal, on the other hand, is overreaction.

Therapeutic Techniques

The psychic self-defense techniques described for Sun/Neptune people are equally valid for Moon/Neptune contacts. Moon/Neptune people are predisposed to emotional contamination. They are extremely sensitive to emotional vibrations, and Neptune acts as a magnet, attracting all the emotional content in the environment. Visualization of the *auric egg* (described earlier) will help protect them from these outside influences. Then, if they experience emotional negativity, it is usually manifested by their own thought forms. The *auric egg* is a valuable technique to use when experiencing stress on the job, and it is suggested for those with Neptune contacting the Moon, and Venus or Neptune ruling or posited in the 6th house.

Any of the above planetary combinations may engender jealousy from other women on the job. Neptune's psychic ability makes these people aware of all the hidden factors before they make business decisions. Other women may resent the Neptunian's ability to make decisions and implement successful programs based on knowledge not available to them. The auric egg will act as a protective shield against job negativity, as well as in other situations.

If Neptunians have become contaminated or inundated with the emotional vibrations of others, they can use water to dissolve and wash them away. All Neptunian remedial techniques are designed to promote healthy detachment from the environment, to

separate such persons' energy from the thoughts, feelings and energies surrounding them. Psychotherapies that use imagery can fulfill
the positive side of Neptune. Gestalt and especially Jungian dream
analysis fit the need.

Female family members of the Moon/Neptune person, are
often so different from the "normal" women in the world, that they
might be labeled "crazy ladies." In past years, most women were not
encouraged to use their creative energies except in child-bearing
and raising. When creative energy has no outlet it backs up and
manifests in anxiety, fancifulness, being "spaced-out," and sometimes in emotional aberrations. Individuals, especially women, with
the Moon/Neptune contact need not be concerned about joining
the "crazies" as long as they involve themselves in a creative process
that they are consciously using to positively direct the Neptunian
energy.

Investigation of the stories within the family of older female
relatives will often reveal women who have been card readers, psychics, folk healers or wise women. In our culture, it is only recently,
that some segments of our population are again recognizing and
honoring these energies. The families of Moon/Neptune people
have hidden the reality of the richness of experience inherent in their
heredity. This often leads to the Moon/Neptune persons feeling cut
adrift from the mainstream of society because they are cut off from
some of the most important energy within themselves. The well-
known Neptunian escapes, including religious or spiritual experience may be more obvious in these people as an attempt to shield
themselves from the harshness of experiencing the world as not
accepting them or as not fitting their yearning, idealized image.
Seeking connections with support groups, in the positive Neptunian
realms, leads to self-acceptance and a greater measure of peace.

MERCURY/NEPTUNE

Mercury rules the conscious mind and Neptune represents the
realm of the imaginary. People with Mercury/Neptune aspects have
unusually creative minds and vivid imaginations. With Mercury or
Neptune in a Fire or Air sign, they weave wonderful fairy tales and
stories because they interpret their environment in a very imag-

inative way. Mercury/Neptune in Earth or Water signs relates more to ongoing everyday life and may not appear to be as highly imaginative; but, these people constantly endeavor to make their environment tolerable by "dressing up" the circumstances of daily life in their minds. All Mercury/Neptune people have a strong streak of drama or fantasy about their lives, as well as the ability to externalize fantasy in a positive way. They sometimes internalize negatively more than they externalize positively and worry anxiously about fantasy conditions.

Mercury/Neptune contacts are often found in the charts of creative writers, poets, playwrights and novelists who write about illusory and imaginary characters and situations. The contact is also prevalent in the charts of musicians, actors and actresses. Mercury communications have a fabulous narrative quality. The contact also enables an actor to take on the subtle personality qualities of the characters portrayed. Even in the lives of more ordinary humans, this contact points to a creativity that needs some outlet other than that provided by daily living. Singing, dancing and acting qualify. Look for other creative outlets if none of these appeal or if one lacks ability. Photography or arts and crafts are acceptable substitutes.

Sometimes the creative-thinking mechanism will generate spectacular lies. Mercury was the messenger of the gods in mythology and his role was to carry messages among them. Mercury wasn't responsible for making any decisions himself and quickly became bored with the job. Since he had great curiosity, he would often mix up the messages just to see what would happen. The Romans called Mercury "the trickster", patron of thieves and con artists. Think of that when you believe the negative thoughts your mind presents to you! Neptune is also quite curious and is not averse to a little deception on occasion. The combination of these two energies can produce some rather dubious stories or tales that lack credibility. The magnitude of the fabrication is measured by or increased by the level of creativity in each particular individual with this contact. It's interesting to observe this phenomenon because these people usually believe what they are telling another person; even if they only believe it momentarily. Mercury/Neptune people may not consciously set out to deceive other people but they are capable of communicating something that is not always completely accurate. Only in extreme circumstances does this contact produce a nefarious type, one who should never be trusted.

Children and teenagers with Mercury/Neptune sometimes try to lie their way out of difficult situations. In an effort to evade the more threatening forms of parental discipline and punishment, young children can invent incredible and highly creative explanations. If, for example, parents come home and find money missing, they will know the child took it because there was no one else at home. But, rather than admit responsibility, Mercury/Neptune children will say, with complete conviction, that a stranger forced his way into the home and took the money. The best way for parents to handle such a situation is to ask the child to tell them a story about a little boy or girl who had no money and then suddenly did. This fantasy technique detaches children from the situation so they can tell what happened and what their motivations were, without feeling afraid or responsible. This technique has also been used effectively with adults in Neptunian therapy. Gestalt therapy, psychosynthesis, and all image-making techniques that disengage the person and provide objectivity are specifically efficacious for the Neptunian.

Although exaggeration is a distortion of the truth, it can be an effective way of communicating ideas that might otherwise be overlooked. People in advertising, sales promotion and public relations, who are involved with image-producing and image-building, often have Mercury/Neptune contacts. This may be an arguably positive use of the energy in a social or collective area. But when people use Mercury/Neptune on a personal level, they often tend to deceive or trick themselves. They see what they want to see, believe what they want to believe—regardless of the reality of the situation. Their thinking and hearing become highly selective. They forget what is unpleasant, discount what they do hear, or listen only to what they want to hear. Their imaginations work overtime as they create a variety of inaccurate constructs. Needless to say, their thinking is clouded, they don't see the total picture because so much valuable information is missing. Everyone should check his/her own Mercury/Neptune midpoint to identify possible stumbling blocks.

Since Neptune views all people as one in a universal spiritual reality, Mercury/Neptune people assume that their thoughts are "automatically transmitted" to others. They see no need to verbalize since everyone else is tuned in. They also tend to forget such mundane matters as dates, telephone numbers, appointments and commitments. They need to develop the habit of writing down information so they won't forget. They can't assume that because they conceived the thought, it has been picked up by others. They need to learn to communicate their needs. For example, if they had thought about telling someone they would be home late, and then failed to do so, the person waiting is going to be anxious or even angry. Mercury/Neptune people need to become "conscious" about these practical details of life that affect others. Since Neptune is the proverbial romantic, it is interesting that these people never forget names, dates, places and times involving love relationships or other kinds of romantic situations from the past. The selective memory censors only unpleasant people and circumstances.

Mercury/Neptune forgetfulness stems from a creative viewpoint. Creative people are not interested in practical issues or everyday details that are not important to the creative process. Their attention is focused on expressing themselves at another level—one removed from day-to-day reality. However, extreme forgetfulness can seriously interfere with careers and other important areas of life. Sometimes this is due to nutritional imbalance. Selected vitamin therapy can be useful in alleviating memory loss or the inability to retain information.

Many Mercury/Neptune problems are reflected in our educational process, in which too much emphasis is placed on the Mercurial conscious mind, on rationalization, to the exclusion of a more intrinsic, perceptive approach. Educational procedures need to give more emphasis to right-brain comprehension. Mercury's abstract logic tricks us into mistrusting these other responses because we have been conditioned to disregard intuition, feelings and flashes of insight. Mercury seeks truth in an orderly pattern through a process of linear thinking. But Neptune brings more subtle perceptions that don't follow systematic patterns of development. Mercury/Neptune people must learn to accept and trust their initial impression, their gut reactions, and not be led astray by the Mercurial mind. Pure truth and personal reality aren't always explainable by the conscious mind.

VENUS/NEPTUNE

Falling in love with love—that's Venus/Neptune. Venus/Neptune embodies the concept of "perfect" love; it is the single most powerful "romantic" planetary combination. Neptune, a higher octave of Venus, represents extreme idealism about romance, love and affection. People with Venus/Neptune contacts tend to project their perfect love "image" onto others. When they meet someone whose personality/appearance seems to resonate with their internal expectations, they superimpose their image onto that person. They perceive neither the person nor the relationship realistically. Everything is seen in the context of their image of love. Venus/Neptune is a love potion, a mental aphrodisiac that dissolves the ability to see the loved one without romantic bias. Neptune lures Venus into thinking its ethereal, otherworldly ideals are attainable through relationships on the material plane.

Venus/Neptune people actually do perceive the other's essence. They can see into the core, where, in truth, we are all united in the same ultimate reality. Unfortunately, we don't live at that level of reality on the material plane. A relationship, fired by idealistic expectations, can last for only a short time. Inevitably, people show their all-too-human faults and failings. What the Neptunian has neglected to see, or has disregarded or excused, is the personality overlay, that includes problematic attitudes and behavior that must be dealt with in daily life. Cross-cultural relationships can occur because Neptune sees no barriers at all.

Venus/Neptune can be one of the most devastating combinations. These people search relentlessly for an absolutely pure expression of love, one that cannot exist in this world. They can be in a state of infatuation, romantic delusion, seeing only what they want to see, ignoring or excusing anything in the loved one that will spoil the ideal future they seek. After a few disappointments, these people may begin to mistrust their romantic feelings to some extent, taking longer periods of withdrawal between romances or marriages.

In extreme cases, Venus/Neptune people experience "addiction" to the loved one. Much of their self-image hinges on whether or not the loved one accepts them. To complicate matters, some

Venus/Neptune people may choose partners who are unsuitable or unavailable, dependent on drugs or alcohol, or currently married. Therapy may be required to break this form of masochism.

Sometimes Venus/Neptune people feel deceived or cheated by their mate or lover. Partners may have presented themselves as something they are not. But, more often, they are perceived through "rose-colored glasses". Even if Neptunians have seen the core essence, they need to be reminded, and to remind themselves, that this has little reality on the physical plane. Once this is thoroughly understood, they may be able to respond to Neptune's higher forms of spiritual love. But Neptune rarely wants to do this. When outraged innocence is aroused, disappointment quickly leads to cynicism.

In the case of very painful relationships, some Venus/Neptune people seek to withdraw from society. An interesting physical phenomenon can occur during this process. Neptune rules the astral body, so when these people are in withdrawal, particularly for long periods, their astral body becomes partly separated from the physical body. Sometimes a Neptunian can perceive this fragmentation in the body of another person. Often the skin has a translucent pallor and the person is "spacey". This partial separation of the astral and physical bodies can also occur in highly Neptunian people who overindulge in drugs or alcohol, or who simply don't want to deal with this level of existence. Any person withdrawing for long periods risks separation of the astral body. Withdrawal may also take the form of hypersexual activity. The person closes down emotionally, and detaches from his/her body, letting it run him/her.

In its most extreme form, withdrawal can be lethal. If it continues for more than one-and-a-half years, people may not be able to break the cycle of apathy. They tend to give up, to give in, to feel there is no hope for any real happiness in love. They will talk about being unable to feel their bodies; they are numb and may want to die. The one-and-a-half years refers to the longest total time it takes a transit of Neptune to exactly activate a point or planet.

Therapeutic Techniques

Emotional illness develops first in the astral body, then filters down to the physical vehicle. This may take years. The emotional state of *dis-ease* will determine the speed of the physical degeneration. Medical professionals have only recently acknowledged that emotional factors can be a primary cause of illness, something folk medicine has assumed for many years. As discussed under Sun/Neptune contacts, one of the fundamental forms of holistic medicine is homeopathy. Homeopathic preparations are composed of natural herbs and minerals that have been purified, not chemically synthesized like most allopathic medicines. Chemically synthesized vitamins and other nutritional supplements may cause adverse reactions and can act as pollutants to the Neptunian body. Homeopathic remedies contain minute, successively diluted amounts of what originally caused the disease. This assumes that whatever makes you sick will make you well—only in different proportions and in different purities. These remedies work first on the astral level, effectively addressing the emotional condition that precipitated the illness. Allopathic medicine suppresses symptoms, while homeopathic treatment encourages the body to cure itself. Homeopathic practitioners usually take a full life history of their patients' mental, emotional and physical background in order to treat the whole person and restore balance in all areas of their lives.

Venus/Neptune people possess a great deal of creativity, artistic ability or appreciation. In Earth signs, there may be a talent for the more tactile artistic activities such as ceramics, weaving and fabric design (although it is not limited to earth signs). Venus/Neptune people are often dress designers, make-up artists, hairdressers, jewelry designers, interior designers—any profession where the creation and maintenance of beautiful illusion is important. These are all areas in which they can bring beautiful ideas into reality. This works very successfully on the creative level where a painting or piece of music that creates illusion can be of lasting value. But, a relationship that creates illusion has little value, unless by some miracle it can survive the onslaughts of life. This will take two fully mature people who are willing to work at maintaining their relationship and at keeping their romance alive.

The spiritual energy of Venus/Neptune can be an enlivening and comforting experience, for both the Neptunians and those close to them. They are able to rise above apathy and disappointment and contribute to the common good by putting energy into meditation, prayer and healing and counseling others. However, if they still believe that personal satisfaction is the ultimate fulfillment, they are in for considerable stress and sacrifice. If they choose the higher expression of personal satisfaction available through a dedicated, transpersonal life, then they have started to overcome the negative side of this contact. People in their 20's and 30's find it harder to achieve this level. Not only are their hormones still flowing strongly, but they need to experience fully the steps leading to the transpersonal path. A "leap" into a spiritual life dedicated to higher Neptunian principles often boomerangs because they may be using the spiritual life only to withdraw from pain.

Both Venus and Neptune represent artistic or creative energy. In the throes of recovering from an unhappy love experience, one will heal faster if personal creativity is channeled. Use the energy creatively so that it doesn't use you!

Seemingly inevitably, the Venus/Neptune person fulfills the old astrological adage of suffering and/or sacrifice. The very rare and lucky ones are blessed with being able to do this joyously and to the advantage of their society or sub-culture.

MARS/NEPTUNE

Mars/Neptune tends to dissolve or diffuse our available physical energy. Even when we can get our Martian energy directed, it often produces the wrong results, something that doesn't encourage self-confidence.

Mars/Neptune people have a well deserved reputation in the deceit/deception department, generally because they're never sure of the ramifications of their actions. They lead others down the "garden path" in unproductive, unsatisfactory endeavors, yet they are relatively unconscious of their misrepresentation. Charles Jayne tells a story about Neptune and the quicksand at the end of the garden path. You are walking through a garden with Neptune, who has no idea about the quicksand. Neptune is pointing out the beautiful flowers and telling you about all the problems he's having. As you get toward the end of the garden, there is a log lying across the path. Neptune falls over the log and into the quicksand. You reach for the log and pull Neptune out, but in the process you fall into the quicksand. Now Neptune, who has, in his unconscious way, inadvertently tossed the log into a tree, is looking around in panic for something to get you out, which he can't find, of course. So you drown. Inadvertent disasters through incompetence tend to occur with Mars/Neptune. It's like shooting an arrow into the ocean. That's what happens to your intentions, your drive and initiative. This incompetence can also invite disasters in personal relationships and business ventures. Despite positive intentions, Neptunians need to more accurately define and to focus their energy, while looking ahead to the consequences of their actions.

Relationships with men may be difficult for Mars/Neptune women because they are consistently attracted to charming, seductive men who are unable to fulfill their expectations. These men may appear strong, but are often internally weak and dependent. Obviously, such relationships are draining, suffocating and demand an inordinate amount of time and energy. On a happier note, these people can also be drawn to men who are imaginative, creative, physically attractive, verbally clever or highly spiritual, even though more energy than usual is needed for satisfactory achievement in these endeavors.

Mars/Neptune people tend to seek soul mates. Each time they become involved, they are convinced they have found their soul mate, which can add up to too many soul mates. What is really happening is that the energy of both people is vibrating at the same level of experience. This doesn't guarantee a compatible relationship on a mundane level, but it can mean they will be able to combine their energies toward some higher goal and assist each other to evolve.

When they are involved in some creative pursuit, Mars/Neptune people, or their partners, may not be interested in sexual expression. Their need for sex is diffused by Neptune, directed into some broader, more impersonal activity. This phenomenon was discussed in relation to Mars/Uranus, but there is a difference with Mars/Neptune. Uranus provides sudden and direct transmutation of sexual to creative energy. Neptune's transmutation is more subtle, gradual and unconscious. The Neptunian's sexual energy is diminished, depleted and surreptitiously transferred into another manifestation. If the partners of Mars/Neptune people aren't aware of the reasons behind this apparent sexual indifference, they will assume they are the cause and may retreat emotionally from the relationship. It is important for Neptunians to be aware of their own sexual functioning and explain the situation so that their partners can deal more effectively with its implications.

There are many Mars/Neptune people with a relatively high level of energy who function quite effectively in the world because they have an incredible dedication to a higher ideal. They are not motivated by personal aggrandizement; nor do they use their energy solely for personal gain. Mars/Neptune implies a need to use energy toward the accomplishment of a higher ideal, beyond oneself, that gives the person a powerful sense of direction in life. The redirection of energy must stem from a serious commitment and not be the result of personal failure. Otherwise, the new venture will prove equally unsuccessful. Sometimes Mars/Neptune people join a spiritual or religious group as a haven or an escape from a personal disaster because they don't want to grow through personal pain.

Eventually the person encounters the same sense of disappointment and dissatisfaction within the spiritual or religious group. It is not possible to transcend the emotional level and escape the deeper emotional complexes before reaching the spiritual plane. Neptunians desire perfection—an impossible state as long as one occupies a body. People incarnate for specific reasons—to work something out on the material plane. (Any guru or spiritual teacher is still an imperfect human being.) The Neptunian wants desperately to believe that a person, an idea, philosophy or system is perfect. They may become attracted to a myriad of spiritual ideologies in their quest for ultimate truth and perfection. Unfortunately, they are continually disillusioned and perhaps deceived by spiritual societies that don't quite live up to or embody these expectations. They tend to reject unconditionally those experiences, and to deny their reality. When a person becomes disenchanted with a philosophy or ideal, it is because he/she has grown beyond it and clearly sees some of its flaws. It is important to remember that the experience served a very valuable function in a person's spiritual development. The spiritual teacher and his/her ideology were not perfect, but to negate the entire experience and view it as fraudulent is counterproductive and embittering. The individual should not deny the wonderful awareness, and development in consciousness and commitment that were present at the initial involvement. When a Neptunian begins to realize that nothing is perfect, he or she has gone as far as possible with a particular philosophy and it is time to take the next step.

Health Considerations

People with Mars/Neptune contacts are as highly susceptible to Neptunian substances as those with Sun/Neptune. They should use caution with drugs, caffeine, alcohol, nicotine, artificial food additives or any chemically synthesized substance. All of these are pollutants and potential contaminants of their physical energy. Because of their Neptunian receptivity and the tendency to "pick up" anything from the environment, Mars/Neptune people are sensitive to infection. Their immune systems are rather tenuous and easily influenced by outside factors. As recommended earlier, homeopathic and herbal preparations are particularly well suited to the sensitive Neptune body mechanism. Dance (or any other flowing body movement) and music will act as a physical "channel clearer", helping to purify the body and overcome any detrimental effects of this contact. Using the muscles (Mars) in positive Neptune ways makes effective use of the energy, instead of letting it passively rule the individual.

JUPITER/NEPTUNE

Jupiter/Neptune represents the gambler, financier, speculator. It can mean money easily won or easily lost. Jupiterian gamblers may have a psychic awareness (bestowed by Neptune) about the outcome of certain speculative ventures. Some mystics contend that psychic powers should not be used to make money, a rather unfair and Victorian attitude. There is nothing immoral about using any talent to make money. In and of itself, money is a commodity. It is "people" who choose to use money negatively or against others. However, if there is an internal belief that it is wrong, then that belief works against a person, and he/she is sure to lose in any speculative ventures. Jupiter/Neptune people can alleviate some of their guilt about acquiring money by using it to help others. Money can be donated to religious organizations, charitable institutions and a wide variety of philanthropic associations. Even buying uplifting books to give to others can remove any possible "pitfall". Sharing wealth or unexpected windfalls with others is a way for these people to reinvest in their own future. People who have either Jupiter or Neptune angular will find their greatest satisfaction in active religious, idealistic, artistic, philosophical or spiritual activities.

Jupiter expands; therefore, its connections to Neptune increase sensitivity, physically as well as mentally and emotionally. All safeguards for the general health of Neptune types need to be observed more carefully with personal planets or points. A tendency to retain water in the system is greater, and therefore, salt intake should be reduced. Addictions, especially to alcohol or mood drugs are much more easily established by people with this contact, and particularly when it also connects to personal planets or points.

Greater interest and appreciation (if not ability) in art or music is bestowed here. An abundance of compassion (even too much softheartedness) and stronger imagination are also qualities of this contact.

On the down side, however, lurks a stronger tendency toward anxiety, apathy and dreaminess, or even an unhealthy floating through life, trusting that all will be well without any effort or plan or even without any purposeful activity at all!

Deep attractions to metaphysics as well as more ordinary expressions of religious belief and philosophical systems prevail. This contact can even indicate true mystics. A great many with this contact can find peace and contentment most easily by involving themselves in a search for inner truth that leads to living from the heart. True ethical behavior springs from a sense of kindness and compassion (Neptune) and justice (Jupiter), epitomized by the most positive expression of this contact.

The most negative is, of course, a reverse mirror image—those who constantly look to take advantage of others—even if this sometimes leads to duplicity or criminal behavior.

NEPTUNE/PLUTO

Neptune/Pluto contacts represent the growth and development (Pluto) of a person's spirituality (Neptune). These people are compelled to grow beyond the material level, promising a great potential for spiritual growth. If Neptune/Pluto people have these contacts aspecting personal planets or points, they may be very effective members of a select spiritual group, relating their experience to others outside the group.

Because Neptune and Pluto are impersonal planets, they oblige people to contribute their energies to the needs of society at large. Any effort to personalize this combination will result in disappointment. This energy needs a larger-than-personal base of operation. Pluto gives power to Neptunian idealism; and those with prominent Neptune/Pluto contacts have the ability to manifest spiritual goals on an expansive social level. Because Pluto rules the masses, Neptune/Pluto people can communicate spiritual ideas to the public in the sense of true service to the greater good. The long-term sextile between these two planets in this century and the next is creating spiritual and philosophical growth, precipitated by the breakdown of systems and structures that society has depended upon for many years. While we are in the crucible of that process, however, it is easier to see and be anxious about the breakdowns. Remember, our media sources report large disasters, not the smaller on-going growth of individual humans in developing towards the light. Enhanced consciousness is the key to this combination, and the price of growth and awareness is pain. So far we have not transmuted (Pluto) our need to suffer (Neptune) in order to grow. Perhaps in a future evolution humanity will grow with joy as the catalyst rather than pain.

When Neptune/Pluto contacts are connected with personal planets and points, the ability to receive messages and impressions from unseen realms is indicated. People with these contacts may be mystics, psychics, magicians, mythologists or psychologists. They cannot rationally explain their perceptions to those who challenge them, even though reams of paper are used in the attempt to do so. The current resurgent awareness of the value of these unseen realms may help us to prevent the repetition of earth's historical negative history by allowing us to integrate a sense of faith and wonder with the mechanistic advances of material existence. War, want and poverty are earth's ancient companions. Expunging them is a step forward in human evolution, predicated upon individual growth in consciousness.

CHAPTER 5

PLUTO

Pluto is the planet of extremes, of intensity, catalytic action, growth and development, transformative or magical processes, death and rebirth, special-interest groups, control and manipulation. It is the planet of Cosmic power, of true magic, the transformation of one thing into another, the unmanifest into the manifest. At a mass level, Pluto represents what Jung called the "collective unconscious". At a personal level, it shows the tremendous secret, interior powers of destruction and regeneration that rule human life. Plutonians tend to experience incredibly wrenching circumstances throughout their lives to promote their personal growth and development. They are tenacious and stubborn and will endure situations that might destroy less hardy types. "Survivorship" is a prime quality in the makeup. Their ability to grow through extremely challenging and possibly threatening personal crises revalidates their strength and engenders an inner sense of awareness of their power that they did not previously have.

Plutonians often serve as a catalyst in the lives of others. When a group or individual is ready for growth, however unconscious they may be of the need for it, a Plutonian person appears or a situation develops which takes the lid off and allows the power to release. This process can sometimes be difficult, painful and confrontational when that which is ready for growth resists the beginning inklings of change. Because this is the most common manifestation, one can easily see where Pluto's reputation for terror arises. The longer one resists the Plutonian need for transformation the more such intense negative feelings like terror sweep the psyche.

When the group or individual has some sense of the need for change there may still be slight initial resistance because of the fear of the unknown. However, once the Plutonian tides begin, the impatient fervor for progress sweeps one into the flow.

The reverse, however, is rarely true. Since Pluto people are in themselves a catalyst for change in others, they need another Plutonian stronger than they are, or, at least, one to whom they will temporarily surrender in order to accomplish growth without extended agony. Without surrender, transformation is only available to them through the trying process of wearing down their own barriers. This may take years rather than the magical minutes or seconds of a "peak experience", that converts the individual to the next stage of growth and development. When this does happen either through surrender or through long-term process, there is a disorientation as one adjusts to being at the bottom of a new level of life experience. The new level of understanding is not definable in words since Pluto is rarely verbal and communicates in an inscrutable manner.

In a personal sense, one can perceive this inscrutability by listening to the conversation of two Plutonian types. They will communicate with each other on nonverbal channels that are perhaps more evocative and meaningful than words can convey. There is always a quality of wordlessness in their interactions; and, often Plutonian people will finish each other's sentences. The Plutonian psychism is different from the Neptunian psychic level because Pluto is never vague or ambiguous. The Plutonian level indicates a deep "knowingness". This type of verbal code is most active in friendships between Plutonians. Their family and love relationships do not demonstrate this interaction as often because they generally will not allow themselves the same degree of vulnerability in more intimate relationships. In daily life, the Plutonian person may encounter a problem involving this secret "knowingness" because there is a mistaken assumption that everyone has the same ability. Unfortunately, other non-Plutonian types, not so strongly connected to this inner channel of knowledge or depth of understanding, will not be able to decipher the Pluto person's secret code. Plutonians undercommunicate on the verbal level because it is difficult to find the exact words to successfully articulate an important thought or intense emotion. They are viewed as being secretive but frequently they are actually attempting to express themselves as clearly as possible under the circumstances.

Plutonians also like to play games that I call the "Hansel and Gretal Syndrome". Pluto walks through the forest dropping breadcrumbs (hints) so the other person can follow. Plutonians always know the whole script but, rather than divulge it, they prefer to give out clues, making relationships a game. If both parties understand this, neither will be hurt, but if the Plutonian becomes manipulative and keeps the game a secret, the resulting confusion and frustration can be harmful to both partners.

The house position of Pluto indicates where we need to bring to light obsessive, even seemingly uncontrollable unconscious complexes, so that the energy can be transformed. Every time we refuse to submit to our darker impulses and direct the energy into productive channels, we strike a hopeful blow for the growth of the species. Transformation should not be an occasional opportunity in life. Daily chances arise to conquer the meaner side of our nature. With Pluto these are represented by power games, abuse of power by ruthless behavior and manipulation of others. Most of these take root in the Plutonian psyche because of a great fear of being taken over completely by others. Stories of a person failing to trick the Devil and thereby losing his/her soul are cultural representations of this fear. What we really fear is our own dark side engulfing us.

Emerging consciousness, the search for significance, a realignment with ancient beliefs and thought processes stimulate our psyche and enable us to take our next evolutionary steps. The dance of Shiva creating and destroying life is one culture's myth that explains Plutonian energy. In modern terms, observations by physicists of the creation and destruction of energy in cloud chambers is another metaphor for Pluto.

Because of their intense convictions, Plutonians often refuse to compromise or yield to others, yet they expect others to compromise or surrender to them. Pluto people have an intrinsic need to control and channel life's energies. Consciously, they strive to control situations, to collect and harness power. But unconsciously, they hope their power will burst them asunder so they can grow through catalytic action. It is the fear of losing control over the forces of life, death, change and growth that gets Plutonians into intense ruts or states of inertia. I explain to them that "The only difference between a rut and a grave is the depth." Some Plutonians are so terrorized by their intense transformative power, they wear blinders to keep it in bounds. By focusing in one direction, or closing themselves off from some people and experiences, they feel they can prevent this power from consuming them. Eventually, of course, it will push through the boundaries we set for ourselves and provide new opportunities for major growth.

Unwillingness to grow, carried to the extreme, means physical death. But any person attempting to grow and develop, in even the smallest way, will receive the transformative assistance of Pluto. This change is like the growth of an emerging plant in the springtime— the plant uses the power to push through the hard earth into the sunlight where it can blossom. The individual who experiences this growth can then come to new feelings and awareness.

Pluto has been called the "generational" planet by Astrologers since its discovery in 1930; and, although this holds for current adults, it will not be true soon. We will see an intensification of "special interests" in the Pluto in Virgo, Libra, Scorpio, etc, people that will not last as long in society since the planet occupies these signs for much shorter periods of time than in Cancer and Leo. Pluto represents the need to reorganize particular "special interests".

The effects of this influence can be observed in the engrossed attention paid to several issues, past and present, by masses of people. Pluto represents attraction and its extreme, repulsion. Most adults today have Pluto in either Cancer or Leo, the signs of biological female and male respectively. The attraction/repulsion of Pluto in these signs has escalated the eternal war between the sexes. Past and future adults do not have the same obsessive/compulsive (Pluto) attention placed on the relations between men and women.

As the Pluto in Cancer generation (1914-1939) matured, books and articles appeared, and there was endless talk from men about the horrors visited upon us by our mothers — manipulation, "smother mother", etc. Every problem encountered in adult life was eventually blamed on Mom. At the same time, the emphasis on female breast development as a desireable characteristic was ubiquitous in movies and the media.

The rise of the women's movement corresponded to the maturation of the Pluto in Leo generation (1939-1957) and was, of course, a reaction to the previous Pluto influence. Now we have books, articles and endless talk from women about male lack of commitment, or too much ego and sex-centeredness. At the same time, there is the "body-beautiful and healthy" (Leo and Libra where Pluto has recently been) movement.

Luckily, the Pluto in Virgo people don't seem to have either of these points-of-view as a motivating factor in their lives. They are much more concerned with work, health and being influenced by monolithic edifices (Pluto) especially companies or attitudes that affect these situations.

Some easing of pressure is possible for the Pluto in Cancer and Leo people by reminding oneself that this planet forces us to grow, and that some of what is experienced is due simply to being "tuned" by nature. One cannot easily change the imprinting in every cell, including the brain, brought about by hormones, even though many changes can be wrought in overcoming upbringing. Perhaps this is finally the answer to those who still struggle with why women or men are so impossible. Remember, Pluto demands unconditional surrender from others. Since this truly isn't possible in this circumstance, we need to turn to confronting ourselves for growth rather than expecting everyone else to change. This need for self-transformation, leading to unprecedented societial changes, is what Pluto symbolizes.

In the occult and spiritual sense, Pluto represents not only the titanic forces of the personal unconscious as represented by gods, goddesses and all supernatural beings, but also our ability to grow beyond our apparently limited "human" capacities through conscious connection and identification with these energies in ourselves.

Since the discovery of Pluto there has been an increasing consciousness about the Universe. Flying saucer phenomena, space flight and discussion about other intelligent life in the cosmos are all manifestations found outside science fiction writing.

A modern Plutonian addition to the pantheon of supernatural beings is "the alien", represented by either inhabitants of other planets or galaxies in flying saucers, or increasingly, by ordinary humans perceiving that they are from "out there". That is, they are reincarnated on earth many times perhaps, but originally from another planet in another solar system. By this, I do not mean the clinically psychologically disturbed person whose alienation leads to an identification with a supernatural being, but the rather ordinary everyday individuals who have always "known" that they are not from this planet. These people usually have this awareness since early childhood, and although there is a long period of getting used to it, most of them eventually relegate the information to the back of their minds and live regular lives.

If the discovery of a planet heralds humanity's readiness for the next step in its evolution, Pluto represents our connection with the greater cosmos, our ability to become citizens of the galaxy or Universe, rather than only inhabitants of our planet. All the emphasis on space since the discovery of Pluto is the way the collective unconscious is preparing us for that larger existence, rather than just a more sophisticated psychological escape from the pressures of modern life.

Humanity seems to be rushing headlong toward some major transformation. Since the discovery of Pluto, change on earth has increased exponentially. There has been more scientific development in the last 50 years than in all previous centuries combined, but our social, emotional and psychological growth has not kept pace.

True to the extreme nature of Pluto, the coming world changes can either be gigantically negative—such as total nuclear war—or, perhaps, can represent the next step in human evolution: living peaceably on this planet and/or expanding into the solar system by creating space colonies. There may even be a non-ambiguous contact with those modern supernatural beings, space people. The

Nostradamus quatrain about "the great lord of the skies descending in flame" may refer to a landing of a so-called flying saucer in a situation that cannot be ignored by anyone, rather than the more widely-held belief that it means nuclear disaster.

Because everything is speeding up and affecting all of us through the collective unconscious, individually using our Plutonian power to transform ourselves in a positive way emotionally, mentally and psychologically can immediately contribute to the collective pool and enable the world to choose the change *for* life rather than *against* it. This would be an unprecedented manifestation of the magical and alchemical properties of Pluto.

SUN/PLUTO

Sun/Pluto contacts combine the personal power inherent in the self (Sun) with the cosmic power of Pluto. Plutonian power is not power in an individual sense. It is impersonal, channeled into the person from the cosmos, and then colored by the energy of the personal planets it contacts. Sun/Pluto people are often subtly aware of this power within themselves and also may recognize the "otherness" of it. Whether consciously aware or not however, this strong influence is upsetting or uncomfortable to such individuals and usually leads them to attempt to control their environment and everyone in it, in an effort to keep the power and energy contained and subjugated. Sun/Pluto people need to mold the people and situations in their lives so that they may temporarily feel safe from being taken over by this "unnameable power" within themselves. They project, and suspect that others are trying to dominate them, so they dominate first!

The fear of power is also the basis for their lack of trust in others and their own secrecy. Trust starts with oneself and if, secretly, one can't trust oneself, then one can't trust anyone else either. Secrecy about oneself means that others can't make judgments about or hold power over one. Most of the time these mechanisms are unconscious as befits Pluto. Managing the inherent power of this contact successfully depends on bringing to consciousness the fear of lack of control of self to oneself and to those most important in life. Bringing this out in the open fully (not easy for Pluto) often leads to solving the trust issues right away. Talking openly about these issues is like shining a light into darkness. Fears often disappear in the light of admission.

People with Sun/Pluto contacts have extremely powerful auras; these are most noticeable in men because the Sun relates to the primary masculine vibration. Because of the strong emanations, these people can walk casually into a room full of people, without speaking to anyone, and literally polarize the activity, creating a space for themselves in a crowd. Some people feel threatened, fearful or reluctant to stand close to a Plutonian. Others will be attracted and surround the Plutonian in a circle, but at a distance of about one-and-a-half feet. This distance is just outside the primary aura, the first and most concentrated area of the force-field emanation. At a deep level, all are aware of the enormous power of the Plutonian, and their attraction or repulsion will depend on how they react to the person's vibration. Even if Sun/Pluto types appear undistinguished or don't display obvious power, their eyes will be alive and piercing. They look as if they can see right through people.

Sun/Pluto people need to direct healing energy to others consciously, or the unconscious may take the line of least resistance and direct energy to hurt or manipulate others. There is a nasty side to this contact that easily manifests in making life difficult for others. Part of this may be to test the strength of others, which Pluto loves to do; but it can also be to get back at others for slights, however real or imaginary they may be. Resentment is a major Plutonian response to anyone interfering with them. Consciously sending positive thoughts and energy to others or to heal world problems translates the dark side of the psyche to the positive creative light of the evolving human being.

The visualization technique for healing others is simply to see them in your mind's eye as healthy, while surrounding them with a healing, pure, clear green color, or the all-purpose white light. To heal the earth, imagine that you are a crystalline hollow column. Bring either sky-blue or purple-black color energy into your hollow body from the cosmos above you and consciously direct it to flow through you into the earth. Hold the thought that this energy is healing the earth and all those on it as you do this exercise.

Up to age 20, Sun/Pluto people may be overwhelmed by their power potential. But the Sun period of life, age 21 to 28, brings increased self-understanding and perhaps greater self-trust.

Sun/Pluto people need, and are really seeking, those of equal strength who aren't afraid to confront their negative games, preferably other Plutonian types. They rarely respect others whose power isn't on a par with their own or those they can easily intimidate. People (Plutonian or otherwise) should never be afraid to confront Sun/Pluto people (even though they may be ultra-sensitive) when they behave badly or make errors in judgment. This will not destroy them or have the devastating impact it might have on a Neptunian. Plutonians respect the insight and perception of others, as well as the strength they show by standing up for themselves.

Fathers of Sun/Pluto children have a powerful effect on their lives—either by their presence or absence, their visible or invisible control. The child's psyche is tuned to pick up the extremes in the father's makeup, his "angel, devil, heaven, hell". This influence can be very quietly stated. Men with this contact spend years getting over the feeling that they can't "better" their fathers, even if their assumption about the father's power is false. The need for a man with Sun/Pluto to feel separate from the father is a driving force that feeds his ambition to succeed in life. Unfortunately, these types sometimes see success in terms of conquering everybody around them. As children they may be bullies, and if they don't learn moderation, they can continue this into adulthood.

The ability of Pluto to grow and develop, however, is often a saving grace. All Sun/Pluto people hold within themselves the seed of an ability to rise above and beyond their conditioning and limitations. The challenge of their life may be to do so.

Women with Sun/Pluto contacts are often attracted to men who manifest power in a negative way by seeking to control or manipulate others. The so-called "macho" type is a raw example of this type. By surrendering their own need to embody power to the man, they make it a negative instrument. As these women become more attuned to their own Sun vibration, they will be able to claim the true power they possess. In its positive sense, these women connect with men who use their personal power and influence for self-transformation when necessary, as well as for the particular world in which they move.

The health of these individuals is usually good. They generally have strong constitutions and unusually strong "bounce back" ability when recovering from an illness because of the regenerative power of Pluto. Unfortunately, some Sun/Pluto people also experience allergic reactions similar to, but perhaps more intense than those with Sun contacts to Neptune or Uranus.

MOON/PLUTO

People with the Moon in contact with Pluto experience intense emotional states characterized as extremely and overwhelmingly powerful. Pluto impacts the Lunar response mechanism with heightened energy eliciting intense and forceful emotional reactions. All of the extremes inherent in men with Sun/Pluto contacts are endemic to women with Moon/Pluto contacts. The emotional intensity is more noticeable in women since it is more acceptable for women in our society to actualize the Moon's emotional energy. Women with the Moon/Pluto contact are more inclined to externalize their emotional power and they have the same dynamic effect on people as men with Sun/Pluto. A man with a Moon/Pluto contact may be attracted to women whose emotional states are defined by extremes, if he is projecting his emotional energy onto women.

Moon/Pluto people unconsciously desire their emotional (Moon) power (Pluto) to symbolically burst them apart because it will make them grow. It is the catalytic action that is so feared and yet is so necessary to development. These people are not aware of their power, nor do they handle its vibrations easily. Initially, they can only contact its strength through observing the effect they have on other people.

These people will not allow themselves to be distracted emotionally which would give freedom to all the levels of the mind which the Moon rules. They focus themselves in one direction and are loath to allow their peripheral vision to work for fear that the power would consume them. Moon/Pluto people can become very single-minded in their personal lives and close themselves off to other people and experiences through letting their controlling impulses get the best of them. But inevitably the volcanic emotional energy continues to increase and eventually breaks through any boundaries.

As the Phoenix-bird rises from the ashes of its own destruction, so too do the emotions and mental processes of the Moon/Pluto person flourish anew after an intense, cathartic release of energy. Fear of not being able to control the unknown keeps them from experiencing renewal to process both sorrow and joy fully, to alter the perceptions and to open the Moon/Pluto to further growth. These people must force themselves deeply into drawing out their negative emotions and go beyond them or they will arise again, perhaps years later, to poison their lives.

The effect of the mother in the life of a Moon/Pluto person is more far-reaching than usual. There is often a pitched, but silent battle waged within Moon/Pluto persons or between them and their mothers. The prize is total control of the person. "Total" in the extreme Pluto sense that the individual's will and soul is subsumed in the will of the mother. Because no healthy human being really wants this, the result is a battle. These people feel that every time their mother (or in adult life, any woman) wants something important from them, it is the opening wedge in the renewed battle for control of their will and soul.

Often the mother will say to the child "You're good enough to eat," or "I love you so much I could eat you." When a Moon/Pluto child hears this sort of thing, there is a shiver of terror at the possibility of this really occurring. Moon/Pluto people's attunement makes them ultra-sensitive to any hint of being taken over completely, a condition that they both fear and find attractive. Fear because it represents loss of individuality; attractive because it is reminiscent of being back in the womb. This is why they will often interpret other people's actions and statements as attempts to seize control over them, and why in adult life they protect themselves from the possibility of this happening by demanding (often covertly) complete loyalty and trustworthiness from others, and by actively avoiding situations that may create emotional vulnerability.

As children Moon/Pluto people also feel that their mother knows everything about them, and even though this can't possibly be true, they resent the intrusion; but also, at the same time, welcome the false sense of security this brings. There is sometimes a symbiosis between the mother and child and this often causes trouble later as the Moon/Pluto person will resist the normal changes and separations life brings, still holding on to this false security. They see normal change as threats to their survival.

Moon/Pluto people function superbly in crisis situations involving others, and poorly in daily life. If their work does not provide frequent opportunities for dealing with some type of crisis, they create crises in their personal lives. Everything becomes fraught with significance. They probe everyone's motivations (except their own) and generally exhaust those around them. Their loved ones can expect either to be ignored, or to have extreme attention paid to their every move, thought, statement and action. Moon/Pluto people's talent for investigation works overtime in their personal lives. Often they can take the heat off their loved ones by finding some study to delve into. If they do find a subject that enthralls them, then typically they will put almost all their energy into that, ignoring their loved ones. These people's hardest lesson is to balance and moderate their emotional and mental lives.

When situations arise in the life of Moon/Pluto individuals that they don't want to deal with—usually involving admission of their negative emotions such as resentment, rage and jealousy; or showing themselves vulnerable to others—they will almost "surgically" cut off their emotional responses. Other people have no idea what is really going on and can respond only to what is revealed to them by the Moon/Pluto person. This infuriates Moon/Pluto people more because they want the other person to read their mind and give them what they need without talking about it. Back to the old symbiotic way of life.

As usual with Pluto, the best way to fully incorporate the emotional (Moon) energy is to bring feelings out in the open. Admit to oneself, and more importantly to others, what is going on below the surface. When Moon/Pluto people can bring themselves to reveal themselves to others, they typically share themselves with very few people, but even this enables them to feel less isolated and less terrorized by the possibility of their emotions gaining a negative hold. The only negative hold is created when they stick to their early

conditioning that their feelings and concerns "are nobody's business," except perhaps their all-consuming mothers.

Plutonian Psychism

Pluto represents the deepest levels of the unconscious and collective
unconscious, while the Moon ties together all the various levels of
the mind. Moon/Pluto people have access to the deeper levels of the
mind. They possess an enhanced psychic vibratory rate that may be
frightening because they can't identify the source of the power.
Moon/Pluto psychic knowledge differs from Neptunian or Uranian
psychism. Uranian psychism is intuitional—information is received
in flashes, like bolts from the blue. Neptunian psychism has a vague,
ambiguous quality. The information is rarely well defined and is
usually open to interpretation. Moon/Pluto people, on the other
hand, possess gut-level knowingness that is always definite and
clear. They know exactly what it means. It is not received like a flash
of insight, but rises from the deepest levels into conscious
awareness. Moon/Pluto people never doubt the information; their
perceptions are not open to question, but they may find it difficult to
act on it or apply it in current situations. This knowledge is Kundalini
power, a serpent power that Moon/Pluto people must learn to handle properly. Once they direct it correctly to heal or counsel others,
the psyche and body are restored.

Magic is another word for transformation and they both refer to
the process of changing something, turning it into something else so
that its form is changed. Plutonian power can also make something
out of nothing or nothing out of something, and this frightens people.

Most people equate the principle of magic with using influence
to motivate other people against their will, but this is "black magic"
and it is simply an abused form of the magical process. A simple
attitudinal change in a person on the internal level is a magical
process and it is indeed transformational. Although nothing material
has transpired, an attitudinal change can totally transform a person's
life. Pluto is nothing, magic is nothing, it can't be touched, felt, seen,
written down or defined. But it is real and that is the power of
Pluto—pure and simple magic. The person merely has to create

mentally the space to allow something to happen and the influence of Pluto provides power for a person to grow, to transform oneself. The Moon/Pluto individual can be transformed while nothing external actually happens. It cannot be defined or analyzed because the conscious mind has nothing tangible to describe or to attach itself. However, the person has experienced it and must not deny the reality of the experience. After the transformation, the person is irrevocably changed. Everything that was there before is no longer present and it is never the same again, after one has lived through an attitudinal change.

MERCURY/PLUTO

Mercury has rulership over the conscious mind, its thought processes and modes of communication and Pluto relates to the deeper ranges of the unconscious mind. A person with Mercury in contact with Pluto has a more direct line of communication and interaction between the conscious level and the unconscious level of the mind. Pluto opens the Mercury channel to the tremendous fund of collective knowledge from the unconscious level that has been amassed over thousands, if not millions of years. The individual may not be consciously aware of the source of this knowledge but he or she will have the Plutonian sense of "knowingness" that transcends explanation.

Occasionally, this contact is problematical for an individual who has been educated into the traditional scientific model. Science, psychology and psychiatry notwithstanding, has only recently begun to acknowledge the existence of the deeper levels of knowledge in the collective unconscious. Man is beginning to realize that we are a great deal older than was previously thought and those who are involved with esoteric philosophies are more comfortable with that realization. The individual with a typical, scientific upbringing experiences difficulty in recognizing and accepting the vast depth of knowledge in our collective unconscious because it is not objectively real or measurable by contemporary scientific methods or the five human senses.

Even so, many scientists admit that some of their breakthroughs came from following "a hunch". This is Mercury/Pluto in action.

These people can dig beneath the surface easily. They probe and research naturally, always searching for more information. They are often persuasive speakers, even communicating unspoken nuance through the mesmerizing tones of their voices. Because of their capacity to always look further, they make good analysts and critics.

Mercury/Pluto contacts indicate communication with masses of people through special interest organizations, involving a group of people who have congregated for a specific purpose of growth and development. The individual with this contact is able to tap into the greater field of information on the collective level and use this knowledge to influence society at large. Mercury/Pluto aspects are commonly found in the charts of people who have careers in advertising, publishing, communications and public relations. It has been called an aspect of propaganda. Propaganda literally means dissemination of information to the public. The negative use of the Mercury/Pluto contact is seen in a person who deliberately lies or deceives people to focus their attention in a specific direction. The Mercury/Neptune individual may deceive people, although it is often done inadvertently; while the Mercury/Pluto person's intention to lie is usually premeditated and calculated. The positive side of the mental power endowed by Mercury/Pluto is observed in people who can influence society at large by communicating the vast warehouse of knowledge that is available to them. Mercury acts as a vehicle for the channeling of Plutonian universal knowledge that can be shared with humanity.

Mercury/Pluto relates to the technique of thought-forming or to the idea that all thoughts have a life independent of the thinker. Once a thought is mentally conceived, it is real, it exists in the Universe and has form. The thought form does not have substance and is not detectable by our senses but is a form of creative energy projected out from the mind of a person. The Mercury/Pluto individual automatically produces events in his or her life and environment through the process of "materializing" mental energy. These people are fascinated with the technology of the mind and will often have an interest in studying magic as a process to bring thought into manifestation. It is not always their full and conscious intention to materialize thought unless they are aware of their own mental process. An individual may be thinking about wanting an old friend to call, and suddenly, the friend calls. The first couple of times this sort of thing occurs, the Mercury/Pluto person assumes he or she is psychic; but he/she has actually provoked the event through the process of "thought forming". Mercury/Pluto people have the ability to create material situations from thought, because Pluto bestows the Mercury conscious mind with intense power for manifestation. The thought is so highly charged with Plutonian desire that it becomes objectively real on the material plane.

People with this aspect, because of their magical-thinking mechanism, must learn to exercise caution with regard to the quality and nature of their thoughts. Their thought energy will automatically seek expression on the material level and Pluto is well known for its potentially vengeful character. When Mercury/Pluto people feel resentful or angry, they may unwittingly entertain vengeful thoughts against whomever they feel is responsible. The repercussions of any thought sufficiently charged with intense emotion can be quite devastating and real when directed at another person. Fortunately, unless the Mercury/Pluto person is adamantly vindictive against someone, the thought does not affect that person. However, if the intent to harm is relatively strong, the negative energy would impact on the other person.

Here's an example. When I was eight years old, I transferred to a new school. There was a pack leader in our class who used to taunt me all the time, so everybody else started taunting me, too. Every day during recess I would stand in some trees at the edge of the playground and brood. One day, when I was feeling particularly vengeful, I looked at this girl standing on a swing and thought: "I hope you fall off that swing and hurt yourself". She did and broke her arm right in front of my eyes! I thought it was no coincidence. From that time on, I started watching what I was thinking *at* others.

The secret of Mercury/Pluto involves the *intensity* of the thought and once it is constructed, it is beyond the ownership and control of the creator—it cannot be destroyed.

The only way to counter a powerful negative thought is to send out an opposing thought of equal emotional intensity to override the first thought and mitigate its effect. This is undeniably difficult since the person must now apply themself to the task of reversing the initial attitude, emotional outlook, and generate the same peak of mental and emotional intensity. If the Mercury/Pluto individual dealt with anger in a more constructive manner by talking it out, the laborious counter thought-forming process would be unnecessary. Above all, Mercury/Pluto people have to discover the power of thought and once this is realized, they can effect growth and development in the most powerfully creative way in their own life and the lives of other people.

VENUS/PLUTO

The combination of Venus and Pluto has been called "the magnificent obsession." Pluto magnifies the Venusian drive for love, affection and satisfaction to the point that these people become abnormally preoccupied with wringing every last drop of feeling out of their relationships, no matter the cost. Pain is an important and valued a measure of the depth of love as is joy. This contact produces an insatiability that no amount of love, affection or attention can fully satisfy. Venus/Pluto people want to be loved fully, completely by "the one". What does "fully and completely" mean? To the depths of the soul — indeed these people even express the desire to possess another's soul, or that the one who loves them would kill for them if necessary. Their urge to know the secrets of the mystery of love can lead them into odd, exotic or even grotesque situations. As with Uranus, the idea is to go beyond that which is familiar or ordinary in the realm of love, but colored by the need to experience all the extremes.

Needless to say, these people rarely find suitable mates! Most people do not want to play at the game of love with such passion; nor do they want to run the risk of being drained of all they have to give, or indeed to receive the overwhelming attentions of the Venus/Pluto type. When Venus/Pluto people think there is a chance that they have met "the one", they inundate the chosen one with exaggerated devotion and attention, often frightening the other away very quickly. In the usually mute style of Pluto very little is actually said in these encounters, the communication is all in the style and vibration of the Venus/Pluto person.

Aside from their romantic lives, these people have great magnetism. *Charisma* is a word that well describes their impact on others. Because of this heighted magnetic charm, Venus/Pluto people are often able to enlist the aid of others in their projects. As long as they feel no romantic impulse, others are drawn to their warmth and seek out their companionship. Venus/Pluto people, however, are tuned to the single-minded, even isolationist, tendencies of Pluto and have very few intimates. They become ambivalent about their magnetism for they enjoy the sense of power (Pluto) over others it bestows on them, while resenting the fact that others expect to get closer (Venus) to them.

Venus/Pluto children are incredibly deeply loving and require the kind of boundless affection in return from the "key" parent. Most of them begin to learn early that their needs will not be satisfied. Those who are denied affection in their early years become obsessive/compulsive. Venus/Pluto people may never satisfy their immense demands for love and affection; they simply can't receive all the love they need from each loved one.

Sexual jealousy, the major negative emotion engendered by Venus/Pluto, usually starts in childhood. The child chooses one parent as the bestower of all they need. Typically, this is the parent that hasn't given them enough attention (remember, no amount will be "enough"). As an adult, the extreme need for attention is shifted to the loved one. Since this is usually the person's sexual partner, the contact manifests as sexual jealousy. Or, Venus/Pluto persons may select one of their children to fulfill their emotional needs.

Venus/Pluto people should be careful not to fix obsessively on any one person as "the only one" who can satisfy their love (whether it is a parent, lover, mate, or child). This is almost impossible to accomplish until full emotional maturity is reached, which may make it a life-long process.

Venus/Pluto in Relationships

Achieving the impossible, attaining the unattainable—these are natural spurs to the romantic, passionate nature of Venus/Pluto people. They are often attracted to unattainable people, those who are aloof or already in relationships, for instance. Or, they are challenged by totally impossible love situations; for example, they may fall in love with a public figure or person whose sexual preference doesn't match theirs. Underlying this tendency is the Plutonian need for intensity through extremes. Only the most extreme situations can begin to satisfy Venus/Pluto people. Fantasies such as the fair maiden rescued by the shining knight from the fire-breathing dragon are metaphors for this impulse. They involve the impossible, death-defying elements to their utmost capacity in their hopes for love which can lead to even more complex or rarely encountered circumstances.

In the ordinary, everyday way of love, the Venus/Pluto person feels the essence of love is missing unless there is a gut-level one-to-one, connection all the time when they desire it.

Venus/Pluto people have the agonizing quality of being unable to let go. They can keep relationships going long after they should be over, and they are able to re-stimulate old feelings years later. They can suppress all the difficult Plutonic emotions—jealousy, vindictiveness, rage and vengefulness—when they are in their teens or older because the parent/society programs them to feel that they aren't "nice" emotions. Then, as these suppressed feelings arise later on, they feel that the old relationships should be rekindled. It's not the relationships that need to be reexperienced; it's the suppressed feelings that need to be fully examined and resolved.

At this point, Venus/Pluto people may find an intense therapy or counseling helpful. After they have reexperienced as many of these feelings as they can tolerate, they may find that some form of sublimation can bring further transformation. Sublimation can be in the form of creative endeavors or alignment with a group dedicated to social change, but intentions must be positive. If they aren't these people will find negativity manifesting in the very endeavors they sought for release. When this occurs, it's a clue that more old emotions are seeking release or that they short-changed themselves in earlier attempts through boredom or impatience. Both may be coverups for the terror of being totally alone. This type of extreme assessment is dramatically satisfying to Pluto types in its intensity. But also, and more importantly, it is only true in the final philosophical sense.

Since Venus and Pluto are both involved with sexual energy, there is a strong need, that can rarely be satisfied, for sexual expression. They may also have rather extreme relationship/sexual cycles functioning in their lives—periods (often years) of romantic and sexual activity, followed by equally long periods of uninvolvement and remission. But, whether involved or not, Venus/Pluto people tend to agonize over the state of their love life. Piave's libretto for Verdi's "La Traviata" has a beautifully intense expression of Venus/Pluto:

> *I have burned with a secret passion,*
> *With a love that is the heartbeat of the entire universe,*
> *Mysterious and proud,*
> *Torment and delight,*
> *Delight of my heart.*

Verdi drove his librettists unmercifully and demanded words be used only he approved of. He had Venus in Scorpio conjunct Uranus, trine Pluto!

To achieve real satisfaction, they will need to go far beyond the personal expressions of love, affection and sexuality. As an outer planet, Pluto symbolizes the need to transcend personal experience. Its contact with Venus represents dedication to something greater and larger than self. Until these people make some sort of commitment to a more encompassing goal, be it political, religious, social or creative, they will continue to feel unsatisfied. It is impossible to satisfy the powerful Venus/Pluto expectations and needs in a relationship with another person. But when Venus/Pluto people become dedicated to a larger ideal, personal relationships becomes less pressured and more satisfying. Partners aren't being asked to fulfill a role only a larger commitment can satisfy. The need to love can then be expressed in an ability to contribute to constructive change in society.

Some Venus/Pluto people, who aren't comfortable with their sexuality, may retreat from sexual expression entirely. People who deny or repress their own need for sexual expression may tend to have physical problems related to the genital area (Scorpio, ruled by Pluto) and the neck and throat (Taurus, ruled by Venus). At the moment of orgasm, the back arches and the neck and head release tension. As fixed signs, Taurus and Scorpio symbolize the process of needing to learn surrender, giving up, the need to let go. This means that Venus/Pluto people must acknowledge and effectively deal with their sexuality. They shouldn't use dedication to a higher ideal to escape sexual dissatisfaction at an emotional level. Full possession of another, symbolized by two bodies fully inter-penetrating each other, may happen on the astral plane (if one is consciously at home there) but it can't happen while we're in the material body. What Venus/Pluto people really want is "soul-meld" with sexual over-tones. Since they may be natural Tantric practitioners, they can achieve full satisfaction through the alchemy of this ancient disci-pline that is basically sex for non-sexual purposes. Read books on Tantric and Taoist yoga for further information.*

MARS/PLUTO

Mars is our energy and Pluto is interested in collecting power. This combination indicates a need to harness, control and collect energy, regardless of its positive or negative quality. Unfortunately, the actu-alization of this process often produces power struggles, coercion and war—negative manifestations that occur because people won't express and process their anger and negativity. Mars/Pluto people seem to be angry at the world and so they collect anger energy, letting it build until it explodes destructively or undermines the struc-tures they most revere. Many of these people obliterate their mar-riages, connections with children or friends, through their negatively directed anger or rage.

These people may also purposely create dissension about or between others or foment discord in groups to feed off the nega-tivity, and then take pleasure in mediating an agreement or solution. For example, a Mars/Pluto person has two close friends, John and Mary. He says to John: "Did you know Mary said . . . about you?" John replies: "Mary would never say that about me." And Mars/ Pluto says: "Well, I don't know, I just heard . . ." Then Mars/Pluto approaches Mary and says: "I heard that John said . . . about you." Mary says: "John wouldn't say that about me." John and Mary start circling warily around each other while the tension builds. Mars/ Pluto just lies back and watches them get ready to do battle. Just

---

*Taoist Secrets of Love; Mantak Chia. Aurora Press.

before it starts, he steps in and mediates. The Mars/Pluto person has not only created the dissension, but can also make everyone friends again (this process is not always conscious). He knows, of course, that John and Mary will never totally trust each other again, and this appeals to the negative, controlling and domineering side of this contact. Even when they don't set others at odds, the Mars/Pluto person often picks a particular person or situation to be mad at or about and lets everyone they trust know about it. Often Mars/Pluto people are not conscious of their game and will bitterly resent anyone pointing it out to them, thereby perpetuating the pattern by finding another person to rage against. They are masters at justifying their poor behavior to themselves. There is a real need to eliminate the internal source of this rage through some form of therapeutic process.

On the positive side, Mars/Pluto people are marvelous organizers. They can walk into total chaos and use their organizational abilities to resolve a crisis. Pluto magnifies the initiative of Mars, so they work most positively within large structures. If they limit their action to their own small world or family, the energy can turn manipulative and toxic.

These people are possessed by an unconscious power urge that can express itself in deep courage and an uncompromising ability to attain an objective regardless of cost. They will work endlessly and intently to achieve a goal.

When these abilities are not harnessed to self-mastery or to organizations that provide the promise of redemption and regeneration (Pluto) for others, the personal drive to do what they want, no matter what the consequences are to anyone, takes over. Then the Mars/Pluto energy turns ruthless and even brutal in the pursuit of their goals.

The potential for the extreme (Pluto) use of energy (Mars) admits of no middle ground. These people's activities are either very constructive or very destructive. If destructive, they can become devious and even make their own rules to attain their aims; and no amount of success or achievement satisfies them. Again, the insatiable nature of Pluto will only be successfully channeled by connecting the drive (Mars) to a path of self-mastery.

Mars/Pluto people have an exaggerated reputation for being involved in violent manifestations, such as rape and murder. But if you compare the number of Mars/Pluto contacts against the number of murder/rape incidents in the general population, you find many more Mars/Pluto people than murderers and rapists. More often this manifests through coercive psychological manipulation.

Mars/Pluto energy is raw and impersonal; it can move just as easily toward evil as toward good. Many people believe that evil is stronger than good; the villain or villainess is always more fascinating than the hero, and often Scorpionic in appearance. We have been seduced into thinking that negative energy in its various forms is actually more interesting and powerful. Pluto symbolizes the attraction-repulsion polarity. People may be attracted to negative energy/situations at the same time they fear getting too close. Such polarities are manifestations of the "collective" polarities in constant interplay inside ourselves and within the Universe. We cannot recognize what is good without knowing what is bad. We cannot experience ecstacy without having experienced despair. All antithetical thoughts, emotions and experiences are partners on the continuum, manifestations of the same ultimate principle. It is easier for us to identify the 'difference' than the constant interplay between opposites.

The Power Drive

Mars/Pluto contacts represent the accumulation and transmutation of energy and power from all sources. The *use* of power is Capricornian, but its *collection* is Scorpionic, illustrating a subtle connection between Saturn and Pluto. Ultimately, accumulated power must be released and used before the circuits overload. Perhaps there are no limits to our power, but we feel safer by imposing limits on ourselves. As we evolve as a race, perhaps mankind will discover these limits are no longer necessary.

The power drive of Mars/Pluto shows the transition of energy from the personal (Venus) to the "quasi-personal" (Mars). "Quasi" implies two levels of intention—energy can be expressed in both positive and negative ways. For example, surgery (Mars) conjures up feelings of apprehension, pain and fear of death. Yet if the surgery were not performed, in some cases, the patient could die (Pluto). This shows the difficulty in making value judgments about good and bad. They are always dependent upon one another.

It's not easy to understand Mars/Pluto on the exoteric level because Pluto is so esoteric. External manifestations often don't appear significant. But when we go beneath the surface and delve into the undergrowth, we can understand the full Plutonian influence. Mars/Pluto individuals who don't externalize their energy build up a tremendous head of steam that will release in ways that are damaging to themselves and others. They need to transform their energy as soon as it starts to appear, to consciously focus it on growth and development in the most constructive and positive sense, either for personal, individual growth or dedicated to some group effort.

Plutonians are often masochistic. They need to suffer before they can release themselves from the bondage of their desires or needs. Here's a cathartic process suggested to help circumvent those Plutonian manipulative impulses that can destroy relationships. Take a small log and a foot-long piece of garden hose. Hit the wood with the hose while you express your rage or anger. Grunts, yells and swearing are encouraged. These help release the Mars/Pluto energy without damaging others. You may, of course, hurt your hand. But this, too, will help, as pain allows release. Hard physical work or exercise is also useful in re-channeling Mars/Pluto energy constructively. Team sports (Pluto and Mars) are particularly beneficial, and team body contact sports ("slam, bang") are especially good.

Other positive channeling of the Mars/Pluto vibration involves connecting the use of energy (Mars) with a higher power (Pluto), leading to self-mastery. Any body movement based on ancient philosophical tenets will serve—Yoga or Tai C'hi. The most effective, however, are those that incorporate either an offensive or defensive (both Mars) use of power (Pluto). The most accessible of these are Karate and Aikido. Where available, Taoist esoteric Yoga is also Supremely suitable for re-channeling the Mars/Pluto energy.

Compulsive sexual behavior is another facet of the Mars/Pluto type. Due to the need for Pluto to experience intensity through extremes, the powerful sex drive of these people is sometimes very active, leading to much sexual activity, or seemingly absent, leading to periods of little or no activity. Both conditions have the stamp of compulsiveness as much of the individual's attention is concentrated on the situation. They can be equally intent about type and style of sexual contact as well.

Frequently when balked in satisfying their sexual needs these people over-sexualize common ordinary life situations. Due to the probing nature of Pluto these Mars/Pluto types will see meaningful sexual content in such innocuous situations as how people shop in the grocery store!

Mars/Pluto people often do not handle their anger openly or directly. Covert hostility is the name of this game. When angry or irritated with someone else they will break a possession of that person, "accidentally" jostle them into doorways, walls or into street traffic, and not follow through on appointments or agreements. In short, they will do anything to show their anger, other than direct confrontation. Obviously, the cure for this is to confront. Due to the fear-of-power complex inherent in any Pluto contact, it is often advisable to write letters or talk on the telephone to state one's case since direct confrontation is too threatening. Once the situation has been faced directly the anger often disappears and conditions return to normal.

JUPITER/PLUTO

Jupiter, the planet of expansion, increases and amplifies the power inherent in Pluto. When Jupiter/Pluto contacts aspect personal points and planets in a chart, the person is able to manifest powerful energy for healing on the spiritual, mental, emotional or physical levels. Although the Plutonian vibration can't be controlled, the person can act as a channel through which the healing energy can operate. Jupiter's healing abilities are represented by the signs and houses it rules: In Pisces and the 12th, it heals the emotions and inner being; in Sagittarius and the 9th it heals the mind. All of our physical ills have their roots or causes on the mental and emotional levels. Jupiter/Pluto contacts often appear in the charts of astrologers, psychologists, doctors, psychic healers and counselors—all of whom are involved in some kind of healing. Even lawyers, engaged to correct some situations, can be viewed as healers. Ministers function as counselor/healers on many levels. These are all 9th house attibutions.

Jupiter/Pluto is a kind of cosmic protection contact, sort of a "God is watching over me" force. Not surprisingly, many of these people are very religious, although they may not be active in organized religion or attend formal services. Regardless of religious upbringing, they know that God (or whatever label they use) is always there, inside and outside themselves, permeating the Universe.

AURORA PRESS

Barbara Somerfield is pleased to announce the birth of Aurora Press, a company devoted to publishing books that catalyze personal growth, balance and transformation.

Aurora Press will provide a publishing vehicle for an innovative synthesis of ancient wisdom with twentieth century resources.

Aurora books specialize in astrology, tarot, the healing arts, color therapy, acupuncture, and the emerging global consciousness.

THE DANE RUDHYAR SERIES

We are particularly proud to publish the books of Dane Rudhyar, internationally recognized astrologer, composer, poet, artist and philosopher who initiated the concept of a humanistic and transpersonal approach to life.

THE PLANETARIZATION OF CONSCIOUSNESS
The Planetarization of Consciousness is Rudhyar's major philosophical work, the concentrated outcome of a lifetime of thinking concerning the most basic problems of human existence and the meaning of the radical social-cultural and psychological crisis mankind is experiencing.
Paper 320pp. $9.95

THE GALACTIC DIMENSION OF ASTROLOGY
The Sun is Also a Star
A deepened understanding of Uranus, Neptune and Pluto can guide us towards experiencing the galactic level of consciousness. The "challenge of galacticity" to humanistic astrology releases new perspectives when applied to individual horoscopes. His new interpretations of the trans-Saturnian planets provide a vehicle to transform how we use astrology in our daily lives, and for the evolving planet we live on.
Paper 224pp. $7.95

ASTROLOGICAL INSIGHTS INTO THE SPIRITUAL LIFE
Astrological Insights provides a penetrating, sensitive, poetic and visual insight into the 12 qualities required for the spiritual life, for Astrologers and non-astrologers alike. Using the astrological signs and houses, Rudhyar builds a framework for impregnating the seeker with an awareness of how to use basic life challenges, as a process through which an individual human being evolves. Twelve exquisite artistic renderings evoke the archetypal, intuitive level of each sign.
Paper 160pp. $7.95

AN ASTROLOGICAL TRYPTICH
In *Tryptich* Rudhyar extracts from traditional astrology a great wealth of psychological and spiritual meaning. New interpretations of the zodiacal signs, houses and planets shed light on the three basic phases of spiritual unfoldment. *Tryptich* is a book to read and reread! Each chapter stands by itself, yet as a part in a vast symphony of revealed values and inspired imagery.
Paper 320pp. $9.95

ASTROLOGICAL ASPECTS:
A Process Oriented Approach
with Leyla Rael Rudhyar
A cyclic and holistic approach to aspects including chapters on retrogradation, rectangular and triangular aspect patterns, seeing the horoscope intuitively as a whole, Yods, an explanation of the three types of every planetary aspect with examples and practical applications.
Paper 244pp. $9.95

PERSON CENTERED ASTROLOGY
Lucid and inspiring material on the purpose of Astrology in New Age guidance and the difference between an event-oriented approach and a person centered view. Illustrated with complete case studies, concrete examples of the holistic approach in action and practical technique.
Paper 385pp. $19.95

THE LUNATION PROCESS IN ASTROLOGICAL GUIDANCE
Leyla Rael Rudhyar
The only book available on the use of the Progressed Lunation Cycle as a tool in process oriented Life Interpretation. The technique, theory, and phases are explained in detail with several whole life case histories to illustrate the use of this valuable technique.
Paper 62pp. $3.95

AURORA PRESS

THE ELISABETH HAICH SERIES

Through books such as *Initiation*, Elisabeth Haich has become world famous for her profound understanding of the human soul. The Yoga schools she set up in Europe with Selvarajan Yesudian have become internationally renowned.

WISDOM OF THE TAROT

Wisdom of the Tarot relates the path of higher consciousness through the color, shape and symbolic forms on the 22 cards. Detailed study of a Tarot card may release instinctive awareness of each level towards the Light. When studied individually, a card may reveal the necessary steps to find one's essential path. Included are 5 color gold Tarot cards.

Paper 174pp. $12.50

SEXUAL ENERGY & YOGA

This book is to introduce the concept of transmuting the physical emotional psychic mental energy people normally disperse in sexual activity for the purpose of uniting their bodies in their higher Self or God.

Paper 160pp $6.95

THE EAR
Gateway to Balancing the Body
A Modern Guide to Ear Acupuncture
Mario Wexu, D. Ac.
This is the first complete modern textbook of ear acupuncture. Anatomical descriptions with detailed charts clearly illustrate how to locate and use over 300 ear points, both alone and in combination with body points, to treat and prevent illness. An excellent repertory listing 150 diseases facilitates an indepth understanding of this incredible and valuable healing art.

Cloth 203pp. $30.00

COLOR THERAPY
Dr. Reuben Amber
This comprehensive book enumerates the myriad ways we can consciously choose to use color to influence our body, mind, and soul to promote balanced health and well being. No other book includes as thorough a historical survey of Color Therapies along with specific applications of color in all facets of life.

Paper 207pp. $9.95

HOW COSMIC & ATMOSPHERIC ENERGIES INFLUENCE YOUR HEALTH
Dr. Michel Gauquelin
A unique exploration by psychologist and statistician Dr. Michel Gauquelin, of the tremendous influence of the cycle of the seasons, range of climates, cosmic clocks, Lunar Cycles, & Sunspots on the complex balance of mental and physical health.

Paper 224pp. $8.95

SELF HEALING, YOGA AND DESTINY
Designed to reconnect you with the Divine, the concepts within this book explain the attitudes necessary for the path back to one's Self. Based on many years personal experience, the author creates a vehicle to realize the essential source of Life, especially in relation to illness and self healing.

Paper 80pp. $4.95

THE DAY WITH YOGA
A different creative energy is at work on each day of the week. In this book Elisabeth Haich has carefully chosen and collected quotations which show us how we can attune to the cosmic vibrations of each day.

Paper 96pp. $3.95

CHART INTERPRETATION —
Astrology and Psychology
Doris Hebel
A compilation of articles on Chart Interpretation, covering Elements, aspects, hemisphere emphasis, retrogrades, stations, parental indicators, and case histories.

Paper 64pp. $5.

SYNASTRY
Understanding Human Relations
Through Astrology   Ronald Davison
This book contains the first comprehensive survey of the various techniques of horoscope comparison.

The author has discovered "The Relationship Horoscope," an entirely new way of charting in a single horoscope the relationship between two people. He also introduces new methods of determining the quality of that relationship.

Paper 352pp. $10.95

AWAKEN HEALING ENERGY THROUGH THE TAO
Mantak Chia
This unique book reveals the ancient Taoist secret of circulating internal energy through acupuncture meridians, for physical, psychological and spiritual health. Written in clear, easy to understand language and illustrated with many detailed diagrams that aid the development of a powerful energetic flow.

Paper 224pp. $10.95

┌AURORA PRESS─────────────────────────┐

TILLING THE SOUL
An Exciting New Approach to Growing Consciousness
Wingate

A truly unusual book, produced and designed to allow new concepts to emerge while "experiencing" reading it. The introduction gives the essence of this growth book: "No one has ever called me a Perfect Master. Nor do I go around claiming to be Enlightened. But I've studied with good teachers. I've done my homework. I practice what I teach. And I'm growing. In *Tilling The Soul*, I share with you my growth practices and the basic tools I use, along with some of the fruits of my gardening. Perhaps these tools and these practices of mine will help you in cultivating the garden of your own consciousness, as they have already helped me and many others who have studied with me at the Communion of Souls. "We are standing on the threshold of a wondrous New Age, the Age Of The Soul. No longer will we seek our truths and realizations outside ourselves, where we have been looking so unsuccessfully for so many lifetimes. "In the New Age of Soul we will find them deep within ourselves, and we will find our happiness and our fulfillment there also." In other words, we will stop looking in all the wrong places and chasing all the wrong rainbows. Instead we will seek first Soul Consciousness, secure in the knowing that all else will inevitably follow. We will become "TILLERS OF THE SOUL."
Paper 220pp. $9.95

CELESTIAL PSYCHOLOGY
Doris Hebel

A comprehensive investigation of planetary energies and their effect on human consciousness, transcending conventional astrological interpretation and delineation. An in-depth blend of Astrology and Psychology encompassing both the esoteric and exoteric levels of planetary manifestation in human behavior and experience. Included are numerous mental, emotional, physical and spiritual remedial techniques designed to assist in dealing with the implications and complexes inherent in specific planetary combinations.
$8.95

SILVER DENTAL FILLINGS:
The Toxic Timebomb
Sam Ziff

A significant and shocking exposé of one of the greatest health dangers of our time. The amalgam used to fill teeth is 40 to 50 per cent Mercury. It is explained in this book how it migrates from the teeth into the body affecting our overall health in a dramatic manner. This groundbreaking book includes:

Mercury in medicine and dentistry
The history of mercury in medicine
The arguments for and against
Do we really have electricity in our mouths?
Measurement of Mercury in the urine
Mercury in the body, where does it go?
How long does it stay?
Does Mercury cause any changes in our tissues and organs?
Fantasy or fact, does Mercury cause psychiatric and behavioral changes?
Micromercurialism, signs and symptoms

This book is written in a clear straightforward manner, ideal for the layman and professional, who wants to become aware of the body of information currently available on Mercury toxicity. Then, informed, each individual can draw their own conclusions.
Paper 168pp. **$8.95**

TAOIST SECRETS OF LOVE—
CULTIVATING MALE SEXUAL ENERGY
Mantak Chia

The ancient sexual secrets of the Taoist sages enable men to conserve and transform sexual energy through its circulation in the Microcosmic Orbit, invigorating and rejuvenating the body's vital functions. Hidden for centuries, these esoteric techniques and principles make the process of linking sexual energy and transcendent states of consciousness accessible to the reader.
Paper 285pp. **$10.95**